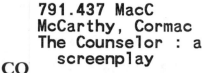
CO

"Like the novelist
Faulkner—Cormac McCarthy has created an imagina-
tive oeuvre greater and deeper than any single book.
Such writers wrestle with the gods themselves."
—*The Washington Post Book World*

"McCarthy's prose [is] the most laudable, his characters
the most fully inhabited, his sense of place the most
bloodworthy and thoroughly felt of any living writer's."
—*Esquire*

"McCarthy is one of the most richly stylized writers in
American letters."   —*San Francisco Chronicle*

"McCarthy justifies the very worth of fiction in the con-
summate breadth and dimension of his work."
—*New York Post*

"The genius of McCarthy's work [is] in its bold, seam-
less melding of private revelation, cultural insight, and
unabashed philosophizing."   —*The Village Voice*

"He is nothing less than our greatest living writer."
—*Houston Chronicle*

CORMAC McCARTHY

THE COUNSELOR

Born in Rhode Island in 1933 but raised and
educated in Tennessee, Cormac McCarthy is
the author of a dozen previous novels and the
recipient of the Pulitzer Prize, the National
Book Award, and the National Book Critics
Circle Award.

INTERNATIONAL

THE COUNSELOR

THE COUNSELOR

A Screenplay

CORMAC McCARTHY

Vintage International
Vintage Books
A Division of Random House LLC
New York

FIRST VINTAGE INTERNATIONAL EDITION, OCTOBER 2013

Copyright © 2013 by M-71, Ltd.

All rights reserved. Published in the United States by
Vintage Books, a division of Random House LLC,
a Penguin Random House Company, New York.

Vintage is a registered trademark and Vintage International and
colophon are trademarks of Random House LLC.

The Cataloging-in-Publication Data is on file at the
Library of Congress.

Vintage ISBN: 978-0-345-80359-7

www.vintagebooks.com

Printed in the United States of America
10 9 8 7 6 5 4 3 2 1

THE COUNSELOR

The counselor's condominium bedroom. The curtains are drawn and it is all but dark in the room. The view is from the rear of the bed and of two figures in the bed. The dialogue is muffled at times by the bedcovers and it therefore appears in SUBTITLES on the screen.

LAURA   Are you awake?

COUNSELOR   No.

LAURA   Okay.

COUNSELOR   What time is it?

LAURA   Two oclock. Almost two oclock.

COUNSELOR   Two oclock what.

LAURA   What?

COUNSELOR   AM or PM.

LAURA   You're not serious.

COUNSELOR   Not entirely.

LAURA	It's afternoon.
COUNSELOR	I know. God you're a sexy woman. What time is your flight?
LAURA	Seven-forty.
COUNSELOR	What are you doing?
LAURA	I'm not doing anything.
COUNSELOR	They're going to take me out of here on a gurney.
LAURA	We could talk.
COUNSELOR	Do you think we should have some coffee?
LAURA	You think that we should have coffee.
COUNSELOR	I guess not.
LAURA	I havent seen you for two weeks. And I have to go back this evening.
COUNSELOR	I know. Tell me something sexy. Words are everything to a man.
LAURA	Okay.

COUNSELOR   Well.

LAURA   I'm thinking.

COUNSELOR   Okay.

LAURA   I want you to put your hand up my dress.

COUNSELOR   You're not wearing a dress.

LAURA   What does that have to do with it? It's something you like for me to say.

COUNSELOR   I know. But it has to be real, doesnt it?

LAURA   All right. I want you to put your hand inside my panties.

COUNSELOR   It's the same problem. Maybe you should just say what it is that you want me to do.

LAURA   I want you to touch me.

COUNSELOR   You want me to touch you where.

LAURA   I want you to touch me down there.

COUNSELOR   You really do.

LAURA   I really do.

COUNSELOR   Say it more sexy.

LAURA   I want you to touch it.

COUNSELOR   God. Are you wet?

LAURA   Yes. Ooh. Baby?

COUNSELOR   God. You're sopping.

LAURA   I know.

COUNSELOR   How did you get yourself into such a state?

LAURA   Ooh. From thinking about you.

COUNSELOR   From thinking about me what.

LAURA   From thinking about your sweet face between my legs.

COUNSELOR   God, woman.

LAURA   Baby? Ooh. I think I should go tidy up.

COUNSELOR   I dont want you to. I want you all over me.

LAURA	Are you sure?
COUNSELOR	Very sure.
LAURA	All right.
COUNSELOR	How did you get to be such a bad girl?
LAURA	It was from hanging out with you. Can I tell you something?
COUNSELOR	Of course.
LAURA	I think you outdid yourself last night. I thought I would never stop coming.
COUNSELOR	You know what that does to a man's ego?
LAURA	I do. Shall I go on?
COUNSELOR	Please.
LAURA	God. Slow. Slow. God. How do you know how to do that?
COUNSELOR	From hanging out with really nasty girls.

LAURA   You've ruined me. You know that.

COUNSELOR   I hope so. God. You have the most lus-
               cious pussy in all of Christendom. Did
               you know that?

LAURA   What do girls say when you do that?

COUNSELOR   There arent any girls. There's just you.

LAURA   But there have been.

COUNSELOR   A long time ago. I dont remember.

LAURA   Yes you do.

COUNSELOR   Do you really want to know?

LAURA   Yes. I do.

COUNSELOR   Okay. They usually would say one of
               two things. Either Oh my God, or
               Jesus Christ. But nearly always some-
               thing religious like that.

LAURA   You're pretty funny.

COUNSELOR   Women like to be amused. Tell me what
               to do.

LAURA   You know what to do.

COUNSELOR   Tell me.

LAURA   What if I shock you?

COUNSELOR   Too bad.

LAURA   Are you sure?

COUNSELOR   Yes.

LAURA   Okay. I want you to finger fuck me.

COUNSELOR   What?

LAURA   You heard me.

COUNSELOR   I cant believe you said that.

LAURA   Believe it.

COUNSELOR   You've reached a whole new level of
               depravity, havent you? I thought that
               didnt mean that much to girls.

LAURA   Depends on the girl.

COUNSELOR   You really do.

LAURA   I want you to stick your finger up me
               and find my spot and push on it.

COUNSELOR   Jesus. Right now?

LAURA   No. On Thursday.

COUNSELOR   God.

LAURA   Ooh. God. Yes. Yes. Ooh. I thought you didnt know how to do that?

COUNSELOR   I never said that. God you are luscious.

LAURA   Shh.

COUNSELOR   Okay.

LAURA   Shh. Oh. God. Oh my God.

CREDITS

Mexican garage. A welder in coveralls and goggles is cutting a line along the side of the tank of a Ford F-650 septic-tank truck with an acetylene torch.

Mexican garage. The tank of the truck has been cut in two laterally and a hoist is lowering a fifty-five gallon drum into the open top of the tank. The welder is standing in the tank waiting to unfasten the hooks and the cable.

High desert grassland, similar to the country around Patagonia Arizona or east of Las Vegas New Mexico. Evening.

A white Cadillac Escalade is parked along the edge of an arroyo under some large cottonwood trees. A two-horse trailer is hitched to the rear of the vehicle and the tailgate of the Escalade is down. The driver's door is open and a man— Reiner—is sitting in the driver's seat looking out the open door with a pair of binoculars. He is well dressed in khakis and sport shirt and he is wearing a pair of tall Gokey leather snakeproof boots.

High desert. Evening. A cheetah is loping at high speed.

A street in Amsterdam, shops, canal. The counselor crosses a bridge. He is dressed in a summer suit with no tie and he carries a black nylon portfolio in one hand.

High desert. A very attractive woman—Malkina—is sitting crosslegged in the luggage rack on top of the Escalade. She is wearing a black western hat with a flat or porkpie crown and a braided leather chin strap. A white shirt with a leather vest and a pair of whipcord riding pants with expensive leather boots. Her long black hair is pinned back and she is leaning forward with her elbows on her knees looking through a pair of expensive binoculars.

Mexican garage. The welder is welding the top of the tank back in place.

Mexican garage. The welder is grinding down the weld bead along the side of the tank with an electric disc grinder in a huge shower of sparks.

High desert. A jackrabbit is racing through the grass. The cheetah overtakes it and kills it in a cloud of dust.

High desert. The woman lowers the binoculars and closes her eyes and presses her elbows against her sides. She almost winces. At this close distance we can see the tattoo of an Egyptian cat at the side of her neck. A second cheetah is sitting chained at the side of the Escalade and it gets up and circles and sits again and stares very intently into the distance.

Mexican garage. A man in coveralls wearing a canister paintmask is spraying the tank of the truck in a paintbooth.

Office of a diamond dealer in Amsterdam. An oldfashioned woodpaneled room. The dealer is in shirtsleeves with gaiters, a tie. He pushes the microscope across the table to the counselor. The counselor puts his eye to the microscope. There is a jeweler's blackcloth spread on the desk between them and on it are seven or eight diamonds, three to five carats in size. The counselor looks up and the dealer reaches and pulls the microscope back across the desk and makes a shrugging gesture with one hand and removes the stone from the clip and places it on the blackcloth and mounts another stone in the clip and pushes the microscope back. The counselor bends to study it. The dealer watches him.

A small Mexican port town on the Gulf of California. Several trucks are being unloaded and are driven along the dock toward a warehouse with a sign over the door that says Aduana. *One of the trucks is the septic-tank truck and it is waved aside and the driver hands a brown envelope down to the customs inspector who puts it inside the front of his coat and the truck drives out to the road.*

High desert. Sunset. The woman is riding out across the grasslands at almost a full gallop on a good Arabian horse. English saddle. She turns the horse and looks behind her and bends low over the horse's neck and urges the horse on. The two cheetahs pass her and disappear in the dust.

Southwestern desert. Distant mountains shimmering in the heat. Looking down a long straight stretch of empty blacktop road all but liquid in the waves of heat.

Southwestern desert. The septic-tank truck is sitting in the chaparral. The driver opens the door and stands up, holding onto the roof of the cab and the top of the open door. The other man watches through the windshield with a pair of binoculars. In the distance a line of stragglers crossing through the chaparral, men and women, carrying suitcases, carrying laundrybags over their shoulders. The standing man takes a cigarette from his shirtpocket and lights it and blows the smoke gently.

Office of the diamond dealer.

COUNSELOR   I want her to have something that she would not be uncomfortable wearing. I dont want to give her a diamond so big she'd be afraid to wear it.

DEALER   (*Nodding, just the trace of a smile*) She
                is probably more courageous than you
                imagine.

*He takes the stone from the clip and sorts another one
and puts it in the clip and looks at it through the loupe.
He holds it to his mouth and breathes on it and looks at it
again. He leans and fixes it under the microscope and leans
back. The counselor bends to study the stone. The dealer
watches him.*

COUNSELOR   Is this a Pillow?

DEALER   No. It's an Asscher. Look at the cor-
                ners.

COUNSELOR   Yes.

DEALER   Let's put it in the grading box.

*The counselor looks up and the dealer reaches and takes the
stone with the tweezers from the clip and takes a small white
cardboard trough and places the diamond in it.*

DEALER   The Pillow has a slight arc to the sides.
                It is a modern version of the old-mine
                cut. Let's look at the color.

*The counselor adjusts the microscope and turns the stone with
the tweezers.*

DEALER	Put it table-side down.
COUNSELOR	So you're looking through the pavilion.
DEALER	Yes. There is more to look through.
COUNSELOR	It appears to be yellow.
DEALER	Yes. This is called the body color. It is still a white stone. But the body color will be either brown or yellow. The colors start with D. The D stone has no color.
COUNSELOR	The colors go all the way to Z.
DEALER	Yes.
COUNSELOR	So what am I looking at?
DEALER	H.
COUNSELOR	Is that still a good color?
DEALER	A very good color. It is nitrogen that gives it the yellow. The truth is that anything you can say about a diamond is in the nature of a flaw. The perfect diamond would be composed simply of light. Do you see the inclusion?

COUNSELOR   No.

DEALER   Look some more. It is small. What we
             would call a feather. Turn the stone
             slightly.

COUNSELOR   Yes. I think I see it. *(He looks up and sits
             back)* So it is graded what?

DEALER   A VS-1. Some might grade it higher.

COUNSELOR   You might grade it higher.

The dealer shrugs.

COUNSELOR   You like this stone.

DEALER   I like that stone.

COUNSELOR   How many carats is it?

DEALER   Three point nine.

COUNSELOR   It's expensive.

*The dealer shrugs. He pulls the microscope toward him and
places a stone in the clip and pushes it back.*

DEALER   Tell me what you see. Remember that
             you are not looking for merit. This is a
             cynical business. We seek only imper-

fection. This is a five carat stone. Tell me what you see.

COUNSELOR (Bending to the microscope) This view.

DEALER Yes.

COUNSELOR The culet seems big.

The dealer shrugs. The counselor studies the stone.

COUNSELOR The crown and pavilion dont fit. The girdle comes out crooked.

DEALER (Raising his eyebrows) Yes. The crown and the pavilion may be well cut each in itself and yet stand alien to one another. Once the first facet is cut there can be no going back. What was meant to be a union remains forever untrue and we see a troubling truth in that the forms of our undertakings are complete at their beginnings. For good or for ill.

COUNSELOR (Looking up) But there is no perfect diamond.

DEALER En este mundo nada es perfecto. As my father would say.

COUNSELOR You are Sephardic.

DEALER   Yes.

COUNSELOR   Do you know Spain?

DEALER   I do. And Spain me. At one time I
                thought that she would return from
                the grave. But that is not to be. Every
                country that has driven out the jews has
                suffered the same fate.

COUNSELOR   Which is?

DEALER   Ach. You dont want to hear. We should
                talk about the stones. The most val-
                ued stone is the red diamond. From
                the Argyle mines. So very rare. I have
                seen two in a long life. A price almost
                beyond belief.

COUNSELOR   I do want to hear.

DEALER   (Leaning back and studying the counselor)
                You do.

COUNSELOR   Yes.

DEALER   Ach. Well. How to say. There is no cul-
                ture save the Semitic culture. There.
                The last known culture before that was
                the Greek and there will be no culture
                after.

COUNSELOR   That's a bold claim.

DEALER   The heart of any culture is to be found
in the nature of the hero. Who is that
man who is revered? In the classical
world it is the warrior. But in the western world it is the man of God. From
Moses to Christ. The prophet. The
penitent. Such a figure is unknown to
the Greeks. Unheard of. Unimaginable.
Because you can only have a man of
God, not a man of gods. And this God
is the God of the jewish people. There is
no other God. We see him—what is the
word? Purloined. Purloined in the West.
How do you steal a God? The jew beholds
his tormentor dressed in the vestments
of his own ancient culture. Everything
bears a strange familiarity. But the fit
is always poor and the hands are always
dripping blood. That coat. Didnt that
belong to Uncle Chaim? What about the
shoes? Enough. I see your look. No more
philosophy. And perhaps Schiller is right.
When gods were more human men were
more divine. The stones themselves have
their own view of things. Perhaps they
are not so silent as you think. They were
piped up out of the earth in a time before
any witness was, but here they are. Now,
who shall be their witness? We. We two.

Here. *(Fitting a stone in the clip)* This is a cautionary stone.

COUNSELOR   A cautionary diamond.

DEALER   Of course. Why not? Although I suppose every diamond is cautionary. It is not a small thing to wish for, however unattainable. To partake of the stone's endless destiny. Is not that the meaning of adornment? To enhance the beauty of the beloved is to acknowledge both her frailty and the nobility of that frailty. At our noblest we announce to the darkness that we will not be diminished by the brevity of our lives. That we will not thereby be made less. Let me show you. You will see.

Evening. The woman Malkina is sitting in a camp chair at a folding table set with a linen tablecloth, with china and silver. An Aladdin lamp burns on the table and she is reading a book. Reiner places a cocktail glass before her with a cherry in it and leans with a shaker and pours a Manhattan cocktail for her. She looks up and smiles. He goes to the fire and turns two filet steaks on the grill. The two horses are grazing just beyond. The cheetahs at their chains stir, one rises and turns and lies down again. The woman sips her cocktail.

High desert. Evening. Reiner and Malkina are standing on a rise out on the prairie watching the sunset. The sun is about half way down. A vast red sky.

REINER	You like it because it reminds you of Argentina.
MALKINA	It is like Argentina. The Pampas. But that's not why I like it. I like it for itself.
REINER	It doesnt have to be like something else.
MALKINA	No.
REINER	Do I remind you of someone else?
MALKINA	Yes. You do.
REINER	Someone you miss?
MALKINA	Someone who is dead. I dont think I miss things. Things are here and then they are gone. I think to miss them is to hope they will come back. But they are not coming back. I've always known that. Since I was a girl.
REINER	You dont think that's a bit cold?
MALKINA	I think that truth has no temperature. There it goes.

The sun flares out beneath the horizon.

Desert. The sun has just set. Bare purple mountains dark against a darkening sky streaked with deep red. The high thin scream of a motorcycle in the far distance, very slowly becoming louder. Very slowly. Then it streaks across the middle distance in a small part of a second, really just a blink of lights, and whines away into the distance and the silence.

END CREDITS

A small and elegant restaurant in a private club. Some twenty tables, the diners well dressed, the women in cocktail dresses and jewelry. Chandeliers, crystal, silver, linen. Over the sound system Anne-Sophie Mutter is playing Mozart's Violin Concerto No. 2. The waiters are in black tie and black trousers with white kitchen coats. Along one wall are eight large oil portraits of celebrities: Bogart, Monroe, Dean, Elvis, Lennon, Miles Davis, Billie Holiday, and the Spanish Formula One race driver The Marquis de Portago. The paintings are bright and quite striking but neither lurid nor cheap. They are oil paintings that look like really high quality pastels. At the far end of the room there is a raised platform—a small stage—and on the platform is a grand piano. The top of the piano is covered with a red quilt or blanket and it is fastened with bungee cords that go underneath the piano. A cheetah is lying on the piano. The second cheetah comes down through the room past the tables. A woman strokes it absentmindedly as it passes without looking at it. It leaps effortlessly to the top of the piano and sniffs the other cheetah and licks its fur. They wear heavy and elaborate collars with black transponder receivers. On the third wall there is a complete Formula Two Lotus racecar hanging from the actual wall nose down. There is a wall of photographs of cars and drivers and celebrities. At the corner table a man and a woman sit opposite each other. He is forty-three and she is thirty-six. They are well dressed and very attractive. A waiter is clearing the table and another is pouring their champagne flutes. He rewraps the towel around the neck of the bottle and stogs the bottle into the tableside bucket of ice and moves on.

COUNSELOR   Anyway, I have something to discuss with you and I'm a bit scared.

LAURA   *(Smiling)* Have you been bad?

COUNSELOR   No. Actually I dont have that much to discuss. So let me just give you this and you tell me what you think.

He takes a small black velvet box from his coat pocket and places it on the table before her. She puts the back of her hand to her mouth and looks up at him. Then she picks up the box and opens it. She looks up at him again.

LAURA   Oh Baby.

COUNSELOR   Will you . . .

LAURA   Yes. I will.

COUNSELOR   Whew.

LAURA   You didnt know?

COUNSELOR   I knew. But I was scared anyway.

LAURA   Good. It's beautiful.

COUNSELOR   Are you okay?

LAURA   Yes. I feel a bit strange.

COUNSELOR   You're not going to cry.

LAURA   No. I dont think so. Are you sure?

COUNSELOR   Oh I'm more than sure.

LAURA   It's beautiful.

COUNSELOR   You are a glory.

LAURA   I'm a glory?

COUNSELOR   Yes. As in glorious. You are a glorious
               woman.

LAURA   Thank you. You are a man of impec-
               cable taste. I shouldnt have said that.

He raises his glass.

COUNSELOR   You cant take it back.

She takes the ring from the box and puts it on her finger and holds out her hand to look at it. She turns her hand to show it to him. She picks up her glass and touches his with it and they drink.

LAURA   Okay then.

COUNSELOR   I intend to love you until I die.

LAURA   Me first.

COUNSELOR   Not on your life.

* * * * *

A small grocery store. A young man dressed in a bright green leather motorcycle outfit—jacket and tight pants and green boots and gloves—is waiting in line, his helmet hanging over his arm. He is somewhat dark. Part Mexican. The woman in front of him has unloaded her groceries onto the conveyor belt and the clerk is adding them up. She turns and smiles at the boy. He is holding a ten-pound bag of dogfood.

WOMAN   Do you have a dog?

YOUNG MAN   Do I have a dog.

WOMAN   *(Smiling)* Yes.

YOUNG MAN   No Mam.

WOMAN   (*A bit disconcerted*) Oh.

YOUNG MAN   I dont have a dog.

WOMAN   Okay.

YOUNG MAN   These are for me.

WOMAN   For you.

YOUNG MAN   Yes Mam. It's a diet.

WOMAN   A diet?

YOUNG MAN   Yes Mam. Well. I probably shouldnt
               even be telling you this. I've tried it a
               couple of times and I got to say it works
               pretty good. You dont really eat. You
               get hungry? You just pop a couple of
               these bad boys. I carry a baggie full
               around with me. Night, you wake up?
               You dont go down and raid the refrig-
               erator. You got a dish of these on the
               table by the bed and you just reach
               and pop a couple. You got your glass
               of water there. Last time I lost twenty-
               seven pounds in thirty days. I'd pretty
               much recommend it to anybody. These
               diets you read about? (*Pointing*) I *know*
               this works. Of course like anything else
               you got to use your head. Time before I

woke up in the hospital. You just got to keep your mind on business. Like anything else. But you want to lose weight? This is it. You got everything you need in here. All your vitamins and minerals. I'll tell you what. After a few days you dont even want anything else. I'd absolutely recommend it to anybody.

The woman turns to the clerk and he gives her back her credit card. The other clerk has finished bagging up her groceries. The boy pushes his bag of dogfood forward.

WOMAN　　　　But you said you woke up in the hospital. What happened? Did you have a systemic reaction or what?

YOUNG MAN　　*(Taking out his money to pay for the dogfood)* Oh no Mam. It wasnt anything like that. I was sitting in the street licking my balls and a car hit me. You take care now. You hear?

* * * * *

Reiner's penthouse. A large room giving onto a patio with a swimming pool. There are about twenty people in the room and on the patio—including a number of goodlooking young women. There are tables and chaise longues out at the pool and naked girls splashing in the water. On the outer patio there is a cabana and a bar with a bartender mixing drinks

*and a large black weightlifter beside him at an outdoor stain-
less steel grill cooking steaks and ribs. In the room itself are
tables and sofas. There are two waitresses on rollerskates taking drinks and food to people, one in a bikini and the other in
panties and T-shirt. One of the cheetahs is stretched out on a
sofa and the other is crossing the room. The waitress pulls up
at the bar and orders two Budweisers. Her T-shirt, worn bra-
less, bears a cartoon of a dragster with enormous wheels and
a huge 671 GMC supercharger mounted on the engine. The
script says:* Injection Is Nice But I'd Rather Be Blown.
*The bartender opens the cooler and takes out two longneck
bottles and calls out Pilsener! and the cook, wearing cut-off
bib overalls, braces himself and the bartender shoves the bottle
into the seat of his overalls and pops the top off the bottle and
then does the same with the second beer and puts them on the
girl's tray and she glides away and pulls up at a coffee table
and sets the beers out and two young women pick them up and
sip from them. On the wall there is an enormous screen which
continually flashes color photos taken of people at parties here.
The counselor passes through the room and comes to a door
where he pushes three buttons on a keypad. He waits. There
is a click and he pushes the door open and enters and turns
and shuts the door. The room is modern and elegant. A bank
of computers and electronic equipment along one wall. An
elegant desk of figured hardwood and stainless steel. Reiner is
sitting on the edge of the desk talking to Malkina, who stands
between his knees. She turns and smiles at the counselor and
Reiner greets him.*

REINER   Good morning, Counselor.

COUNSELOR   Morning.

Malkina leans and whispers into Reiner's ear and pats him on the knee and turns to go. She is tall, dark, and very attractive. She smiles again at the counselor as she passes him.

MALKINA   Hola, Guapo.

COUNSELOR   Hey.

She goes out and closes the door and Reiner gets off of the desk and turns his leather swivel-chair and sits in it and motions the counselor to a leather sofa at the end of the desk and at right angles to it. The counselor comes over and sits down.

REINER   How's the bride?

COUNSELOR   Bridal.

REINER   That sounds about right. Nice lady. I assume she's not privy to your newest business venture.

COUNSELOR   She's not. And your lady?

REINER   Yeah.

COUNSELOR   Yeah what.

REINER   She's fine. I dont know what she knows.
              I dont want to know.

COUNSELOR   You dont trust her.

REINER   Jesus, Counselor. She's a woman.

COUNSELOR   Woo.

REINER   Yeah, well. I dont mean it to sound
              that cold. I just mean that where men
              are concerned they've got their own
              agenda. I always liked smart women.
              But it's been an expensive hobby.

COUNSELOR   Yeah. *(Nodding toward the electronic wall)*
              Do you know what all that stuff is?

REINER   Mostly. Anything I dont know I can ask
              her. Which worries me even more.

COUNSELOR   Mmm.

REINER   Yeah.

COUNSELOR   You never told me what happened with
              you and the lovely Clarissa.

REINER   Miss Clarissa. Of the extraordinary
              body. What happened? I think in the
              end it was jealousy that undid us.

COUNSELOR   Jealousy?

REINER   Yeah. She was getting more pussy than I was.

COUNSELOR   *(Smiling)* Is that true?

REINER   I dont know. Probably. I have to say that for a girl who liked girls she took an extraordinary interest in the male member. She sucked on it so hard it finally corrected my vision. She left me for this goodlooking black woman. Had a boyfriend used to play for the Oilers. Nice chap. We met once for drinks at a club in Dallas to discuss our mutual plight. He was taking it rather poorly, I have to say. Women do better, dont they?

COUNSELOR   Maybe they have more practice at it.

REINER   Yeah, well. My guess is that in most cases if you still had the woman you're weeping over you'd be weeping harder.

COUNSELOR   *(Smiling)* You cant hear anything in here, can you?

REINER   It's better than that.

COUNSELOR   Yeah?

REINER   You cant hear anything out there.

COUNSELOR   So is this place secure?

REINER   Who knows? I dont speak in arraignable
              phrases anywhere. There's a scrambler
              on the phone but still there's a lot of
              smart people out there. Of course any-
              body who thinks he's the smartest is on
              his way to the slam.

COUNSELOR   Would that be me?

REINER   Nah. Although I have to say that I
              always did think a law degree was a
              license to steal. And that you for one
              hadnt really capitalized on it.

The counselor shrugs.

REINER   Yeah. Well, you're not the straight dude
              people think though, are you?

COUNSELOR   I guess not.

REINER   I dont mean the caper. I mean you.
              Women like you.

COUNSELOR   All right.

REINER   You know what they like about you?

COUNSELOR   I'm a good fuck?

REINER   Yeah, right. They can sniff out the
                moral dilemma. The paradox.

COUNSELOR   Moral dilemma.

REINER   Yeah. They're drawn to it. Not sure
                why. Maybe it's just that lacking any
                moral sense themselves they're fas-
                cinated by it in men. You think about
                it. You want to know if a guy has
                issues watch the way women react to
                him.

COUNSELOR   Interesting.

REINER   Men are attracted to flawed women too
                of course, but their illusion is that they
                can fix them. Women dont want to fix
                anything. They just want to be enter-
                tained. The truth about women is you
                can do anything to them except bore
                them.

COUNSELOR   Well, there's nothing about Laura that
                I would want to fix.

REINER   Maybe not.

COUNSELOR	But you think she probably knows things about me that I dont know about myself.
REINER	Jesus, Counselor. I'm not even sure what sort of a question that is.
COUNSELOR	Yeah. And you? Vis-à-vis your inamorata.
REINER	You dont want to know. I dont want to know.
COUNSELOR	Moral dilemmas.
REINER	Yeah. You pursue this road that you've embarked upon and you will eventually come to moral decisions that will take you completely by surprise. You wont see it coming at all.
COUNSELOR	Such as?
REINER	Such as whether to waste somebody. Or have them wasted.
COUNSELOR	You ever been faced with a decision like that?
REINER	You're a member of the court.

COUNSELOR	Well. I dont intend to take this up as a trade.
REINER	One-time deal. Right?
COUNSELOR	Which you've heard a thousand times.
REINER	No. But a few. What usually happens is that after a couple of deals they know more than you do and they set up shop across the street.
COUNSELOR	How does that work out for them?
REINER	Not well.
COUNSELOR	So would that be a moral issue?
REINER	Not for me.
COUNSELOR	Or for your associates.
REINER	Yeah well. They have a real aversion to mixing business with pleasure. Do you know what a bolito is?
COUNSELOR	No. A bolo is one of those skinny neckties. Or is it one of those things you throw? Argentina.

REINER	Yeah. In this case it's a mechanical device. It has this small electric motor with this rather incredible compound gear that retrieves a steel cable. Battery-driven. The cable is made out of some unholy alloy, almost impossible to cut it, and it's in a loop, and you come up behind the guy and drop it over his head and pull the free end of the cable tight and walk away. No one even sees you. Pulling the cable activates the motor and the noose starts to tighten and it continues to tighten until it goes to zero.
COUNSELOR	It cuts the guy's head off.
REINER	It can.
COUNSELOR	There's nothing he can do.
REINER	No.
COUNSELOR	Jesus.
REINER	Yeah.
COUNSELOR	How long does it take?
REINER	Three, four minutes. Five maybe. It depends on your collar size.

COUNSELOR   You're shitting me.

REINER   Nope. Mostly wretched excess of course. It's just that there'd be no easy way to turn the thing off. Or reason to. It just keeps running until the noose closes completely and then it self-destructs. Actually you're probably dead in less than a minute.

COUNSELOR   From strangulation.

REINER   No. The wire cuts through the carotid arteries and sprays blood all over the spectators and then everybody goes home.

COUNSELOR   Jesus.

REINER   Yeah, well.

COUNSELOR   Bolito.

REINER   Yeah. Probably a play on words too. Boleto—with an e—is the spanish word for ticket. As in yours has just been punched.

COUNSELOR   I wouldnt think it would go through bone.

REINER   It wont. It would have to go between
              the vertebrae. The gear is a worm drive
              with a gain built into it. Or a reduction,
              actually. It keeps getting stronger and
              slower. To compensate for the com-
              pression of the tissue.

COUNSELOR   How do you know all this?

REINER   You know how I like gadgets. Any-
              way, a friend of mine got hold of one.
              In Calexico. Stolen out of County
              Property.

COUNSELOR   I would think they'd be expensive.

REINER   They are. This one was used.

COUNSELOR   Sweet.

Reiner shrugs.

COUNSELOR   Why does no one see him?

REINER   See who?

COUNSELOR   The garroteer.

REINER   Oh. Well, given a choice between
              watching someone walk away down

the street and watching someone being slowly decapitated by a device apparently engineered and patented in the halls of hell you are going to watch the latter. That's just the way it is. You may think you should avert your gaze. But you wont.

COUNSELOR   Where's all this beheading shit come from? You never used to see that.

REINER   Yeah. It's blown in here from the East.

COUNSELOR   Meaning the East.

REINER   Yeah. You put nine Mexicans and an Arab in a room and give them each a hundred dollars and come back in a couple of hours who do you think is going to be holding the grand?

COUNSELOR   So are you gearing up to do business with them down the road?

REINER   The Arabs?

COUNSELOR   Yeah.

REINER   No.

COUNSELOR   Why is that?

REINER   Because they dont need your money.

* * * * *

Southwestern desert. The septic-tank truck and a pickup are parked in the chaparral. The two Mexican drivers are talking to two other men. They squat on the ground. One passes around a pack of cigarettes. Then he picks up a stick and draws a map in the dirt.

* * * * *

A warehouse with floodlights. The metal door clanks upward and the green leather cyclist comes whining through on a Kawasaki ZX-12 and brakes and does a donut on the concrete floor and stops and shuts off the bike and takes off his helmet. A doberman runs to him and stands up and he hugs her and tousles her ears and steps off of the bike. There is a black late-model Cadillac Escalade parked toward the rear of the warehouse. He crosses the room with her leaping about him to an island in the far corner that contains a kitchen and a bed, a tin locker, a leather easy chair—taking the bag of dogfood with him. He fixes her bowl of food and turns on the stereo and opens the refrigerator and takes out a frozen dinner and puts it in the microwave and opens a beer and sits, watching the dog eat. He puts the beer on the table and stands up and takes off the leather jacket and unzips a pocket and takes out a clear plastic bag and pitches it onto the table. It is full of hundred dollar bills. He opens a drawer and takes out a packet of marijuana and papers and sits rolling a joint. He lights it and leans back with his eyes closed. The dog finishes her dish and comes over and circles and sniffs and sneezes. He blows smoke at her and she sneezes and circles.

YOUNG MAN   Yeah, well. Too bad.

The timing bell rings on the microwave. He gets up and goes over and opens the door and takes out the meal. The dog sits watching.

YOUNG MAN   You dont eat lasagna. Go lie down.

* * * * *

In the club. The counselor and Laura at a table. A young man in a T-shirt, sportcoat, and jeans, with a girl, on their way out. They stop and he pulls back from the girl and smiles at the counselor.

TONY   Well Counselor, how are you making it?

The counselor leans back and studies him.

COUNSELOR   I'm all right.

TONY   Is this your lady?

COUNSELOR   It is.

TONY	How are you, Mam?
LAURA	I'm fine. Thank you.
TONY	Me and the counselor go back a ways. Dont we, Counselor?
COUNSELOR	We do. I'm afraid.
TONY	Dont be afraid, Counselor. Hell, I'm okay with everything. You okay with everything, Counselor?
COUNSELOR	I am if you are.
TONY	*(Addressing Laura)* See there? Aint he just the best son of a bitch?
GIRL	Come on, Tony.
TONY	How long you know this guy, Petunia?
LAURA	Long enough.
TONY	Long enough? How long is that, long enough?
COUNSELOR	Maybe you should listen to your lady friend.
TONY	Is that what you do, Counselor?

COUNSELOR	Pretty much.
TONY	Does he keep you entertained?
LAURA	That's none of your business.
TONY	Because you look to me like you might get bored easy.
GIRL	Tony. Let's go.
TONY	Okay. I'm gone. Here. Let me try this one on you. See if you can tell me what this is. This is pretty good.

He pulls up his T-shirt and places his hands palm down on either side of his navel and moves the skin of his stomach up and down alternately six or eight times very quickly and then spreads them to show his navel. Then he does it again.

TONY	You get it?

Laura has turned away with her eyes closed.

TONY	Let me show you again. Watch.

He repeats the performance.

TONY	Come on, Counselor. It's a girl runnin the hurdles.

Laura bows her head, her eyes closed.

TONY   Come on, Sugardumplin. What? You
                dont think that's funny? She's a little
                up tight aint she Counselor?

The counselor pushes back his chair and stands.

GIRL   Tony I'm going.

TONY   Hell, Counselor. Keep your seat. You
                dont have to get up for me. You know,
                Petunia, the counselor here has got a
                way of sullin up like a possum when he
                dont get his way. I'm goin to say that
                you have probably noticed it. But that
                aint really the problem. The real prob-
                lem is that his thin skin makes it okay
                in his eyes for you to wind up under the
                bus. You know what I'm sayin? Any-
                way, that's how I see it. *(He holds up his
                hands)* All right. I'm goin. I'm goin. You
                take care now. You hear?

                      *   *   *   *   *

*A cafe in a shopping mall. Malkina and Laura are at a table
having lunch.*

MALKINA   So how many carats is it?

44

LAURA	I dont know.
MALKINA	*(Pausing with a forkful of salad, then putting it down again)* You dont know.
LAURA	*(Smiling)* No.
MALKINA	You have got to be kidding me.
LAURA	No.
MALKINA	Let me see it.

Laura holds out her hand.

MALKINA	No. Take it off.

Laura takes off the ring and hands it across the table to her. Malkina looks at the ring, turns it, holds it up to the light. She hands it back.

MALKINA	It's a three and half carat. Maybe a three point eight. Nice stone. Asscher cut.
LAURA	*(Putting the ring back on)* Thank you.
MALKINA	Good color. Probably an F or a G. Nothing visible so it's at least a VS-2. Do you want to know what it's worth?

LAURA   No.

MALKINA   *(Smiling and shaking her head, stabbing at her salad)* You really dont, do you?

LAURA   No.

MALKINA   So have you set a date?

LAURA   No. I want to get married in the Church. Which he says is all right. He's been married before and I thought that would be a problem but the Church doesnt recognize other marriages. Anyway, I'm looking for a job here.

MALKINA   Are you scared?

LAURA   *(Smiling)* No. A bit nervous. Sometimes.

MALKINA   Are you a church lady?

LAURA   I go. Yes. It's important to me.

MALKINA   What about confession?

LAURA   Yes. Well, maybe not so much.

MALKINA   Does the priest ask you about sex?

LAURA	He doesnt ask. But you're supposed to tell him everything.
MALKINA	He doesnt press you for the juicy details?
LAURA	*(Smiling)* No.
MALKINA	He touched me, Father. Where, my child? In the back seat, Father. But you're supposed to go, right?
LAURA	Yes. So you can go to communion.
MALKINA	And whatever nasty shit you did you're supposed to promise not to do it again.
LAURA	Yes.
MALKINA	*(Shaking her head)* Mmm. What if a non-Catholic went in to confess? What would he do?
LAURA	I dont know. Why would you?
MALKINA	I dont know. Maybe because you're only as sick as your secrets. Would he listen?
LAURA	I dont know. He wouldnt be able to give you absolution if you're not a Catholic.

MALKINA   You believe that only Catholics go to
            heaven?

LAURA   I think it's pretty much what the
            Church teaches. I'm not so sure.

MALKINA   Yeah. But anybody could just wander
            into the booth, right?

LAURA   The confessional? Yes. I suppose.

MALKINA   So what do you say?

LAURA   You confess your sins.

MALKINA   Yes, but what do you say? You get in
            there and what? Do you tell him who
            you are?

LAURA   No. You say: Bless me Father for I have
            sinned. And you say how long it's been
            since your last confession. And then
            you tell him what you've done. Then
            when you're through you say that you're
            sorry. Heartily sorry, you say. And that
            you wont do it again.

MALKINA   But you do.

LAURA   I suppose. Usually.

MALKINA	Do you give him any money or anything?
LAURA	No.
MALKINA	*(Shaking her head)* Mmm. Strange. Suppose you've done something really nasty. He doesnt pump you for details?
LAURA	I dont think so. You're embarrassing me.
MALKINA	I can see. You're blushing. Okay. We'll change the subject.
LAURA	Good.
MALKINA	We'll talk about *my* sex life.
LAURA	*(Looking up)* You're teasing.
MALKINA	Just rattling your cage. What a world.
LAURA	You think the world is strange.
MALKINA	I meant yours.

* * * * *

Northern Mexico at US border. Night. The septic-tank truck is lumbering over the desert, driving with only the parking

*lights on at the front of the truck. The truck crests a slight
rise and grinds to a halt. In the distance are the lights of a city
along the horizon.*

* * * * *

*A bar at the edge of the city. Afternoon. The counselor comes
in and stands at the door for a moment to accustom his eyes to
the darkness. Westray is sitting at a table in the corner and he
raises one hand. The counselor crosses the room and pulls back
a chair and sits at the table. Westray is slightly older than the
counselor, nice looking and well dressed. There are very few
customers in the bar. At the far end a young man is playing
the pinball machine and he gives it a shove and tilts it and
walks away. Westray is wearing dark glasses.*

WESTRAY   Counselor.

COUNSELOR   It's not dark enough in here for you?

Westray removes the glasses to reveal a black eye.

COUNSELOR   Wow. That's a dandy. What happened?

WESTRAY   Confrontation with a doorman. Who
                        bore a disquieting resemblance to Pro-
                        consul.

COUNSELOR   A confrontation?

Westray shrugs.

COUNSELOR   Jesus. What did you say to him?

WESTRAY   I think I told him that he was not to take it personally but that he should go fuck himself.

COUNSELOR   But not to take it personally.

WESTRAY   No.

COUNSELOR   What did he say?

WESTRAY   He said: I'm going to hurt you, White Person. Here she is.

A waitress has arrived at the table. She puts down paper napkins.

WAITRESS   What'll it be?

WESTRAY   I'll have a Heineken.

COUNSELOR   Make it two.

The waitress glances at Westray's eye and moves away. Westray sits back in his chair and studies the counselor.

COUNSELOR   I didnt know that you got into donny-brooks.

WESTRAY   I dont. Anyway, that was in another country.

COUNSELOR	And besides the wretch is dead?
WESTRAY	No. But I've sent a pair of reliable chaps to talk to him. Bloody expensive, too.
COUNSELOR	You surprise me.
WESTRAY	You shouldnt be surprised, Counselor. What's the Miller quote that Reiner likes? The smallest crumb can devour us? You learn to let nothing pass. You cant afford to.
COUNSELOR	I should keep that in mind?
WESTRAY	You might keep that in mind. So. Fire away.
COUNSELOR	All right. What do you do with the money?
WESTRAY	What do I do or what does one do?
COUNSELOR	You.
WESTRAY	Mine goes off shore. We can talk if you like. But you cant use my people.
COUNSELOR	All right.
WESTRAY	Let me make a call.

COUNSELOR   All right.

WESTRAY   What else. You're not happy.

COUNSELOR   I'm all right. What's the buy-out for
             this whole deal?

WESTRAY   Net net?

COUNSELOR   Funny. Yeah. Net net.

WESTRAY   Hard to put a cold dollar on it. You
             dont know what your expenses are up
             front. It's six hundred and twenty-five
             kilos. Pure uncut. It goes for about fifty
             dollars an ounce in Colombia and the
             street price in Dallas can be as high as
             two grand.

COUNSELOR   Is that where it's going? Dallas?

WESTRAY   No. It's going to Chicago. If the whole
             deal were to go tits up in a ditch the
             papers would put the street value at a
             hundred mil. We're probably looking at
             twenty. Maybe a bit more.

The counselor gets out his pen and starts to write on the napkin.

WESTRAY   It's twenty-one thousand nine hundred
             ounces.

COUNSELOR   (*Leaning back and studying Westray*) You
             do that in your head?

WESTRAY   No. I just remembered it. I know
             somebody who could do it in her head
             though.

COUNSELOR   Yeah. I'll bet you're right.

WESTRAY   If you're not in, you need to tell me.

COUNSELOR   I'm all right.

WESTRAY   It's not just our people. You've got the
             money guys. You have to get cash in
             dollars into Mexico and then they have
             to get it out again. But that's all they do.
             You have to use US banks. This means
             you have to have a corporation. And
             even then you have to have someone
             on the inside. You'd be surprised at the
             people who are in this business. Very
             surprised.

COUNSELOR   Do you have a corporation?

WESTRAY   No. Of course not. We just pay the
             points. The other option of course is
             cash. Which an even bigger head-
             ache. For all the obvious reasons. The
             biggest issue is not that your man is

going to fall in love with a poledancer and go south with your ducats. The biggest issue is that somebody is going to figure out who he is and what he's up to. Here we go.

The waitress arrives and sets down the bottles and glasses. The counselor takes a clip of bills from his front pocket but Westray already has a twenty out and he puts it on the tray. She reaches in her apron pocket for change.

WESTRAY   You're good.

WAITRESS   *(Surprised, smiling)* Well thank you.

WESTRAY   I dont suppose you have any pilsener glasses back there.

WAITRESS   Any what?

WESTRAY   It's all right. Thanks.

The waitress moves away.

WESTRAY   I see your look. I like to tip them enough that they dont thank you.

COUNSELOR   Why dont they thank you?

WESTRAY   Because they think it's a mistake. And they dont want to call attention to it.

COUNSELOR (*Shaking his head and smiling*) Well. Cheers.

WESTRAY I dont like to be wrong about human nature. Anyway (*Tipping his bottle toward the counselor*) a plague of pustulant boils upon all their scurvid asses.

COUNSELOR (*Smiling*) Is that your normal toast?

WESTRAY Increasingly.

COUNSELOR (*Smiling*) If the drug wars stop this will dry up, right?

WESTRAY Let's just say it will be more risky. That's the part that Reiner doesnt seem to get. You may have noticed that his lifestyle has become increasingly lavish.

COUNSELOR I've noticed.

WESTRAY I never go in his club. And I miss the bastard. We always shared a taste for exotic women. A few times in fact shared the women themselves.

COUNSELOR That wouldnt include the present one would it?

Westray leans back and studies the counselor.

WESTRAY   And why would you ask me that?

COUNSELOR   No reason. Sorry.

WESTRAY   I see a murky picture forming in your
               mind. How well do you know her?

COUNSELOR   Not all that well. Why?

WESTRAY   Because you dont know someone until
               you know what they want. Is why.

COUNSELOR   I'll try and remember that.

WESTRAY   Good.

COUNSELOR   And you're advising me to travel light.

WESTRAY   Yes.

COUNSELOR   And Reiner?

WESTRAY   Reiner thinks that nothing bad can
               happen. He's in love. Any of this sound
               familiar? You guys are opening a new
               club.

COUNSELOR   Is that okay?

WESTRAY   Sure. What the fuck. What else?

COUNSELOR   I dont know.

WESTRAY   Do you know how many people were killed in Juarez last year?

COUNSELOR   No. A lot.

WESTRAY   Yes. I think three thousand is a lot. These people are another species, Counselor. You might want to think about that as well. They will rip out your liver and eat it in front of your dog.

COUNSELOR   Jesus, Westray.

WESTRAY   Let me ask you this. Before the so-called drug wars who do you think was killing all those young girls in Juarez?

COUNSELOR   I dont know. Nobody knows.

WESTRAY   Nobody knows.

COUNSELOR   No.

WESTRAY   Come on, Counselor. Hundreds of young girls? Thousands, most likely. Follow the money. If you have so much cash that you're using it to insulate your house and you've bought all the cars and clothes and guns that you can find a place to put, and you are morally depraved beyond all human recognition, what then do you spend your money on?

COUNSELOR   Why do they kill them?

WESTRAY   Who knows. For fun. Snuff films. You'll see. Those will start turning up. Anyway, what do you do with a fifteen year old girl that you've just violated with a tiretool?

COUNSELOR   You think the drug lords hire kidnappers to keep them supplied with young girls.

WESTRAY   I think they have kidnappers on full retainer.

COUNSELOR   I guess I should think about that too.

WESTRAY   I cant advise you, Counselor.

COUNSELOR   Yeah. But you are advising me.

WESTRAY   I just want you to be sure that you're locked in. I dont know. Maybe I should tell you what Mickey Rourke told what's-his-face. That that's my recommendation anyway. Dont do it.

COUNSELOR   *(Smiling)* Because I'll tell you something, Counselor. This arson is a serious crime.

WESTRAY   Yes. And so is this.

COUNSELOR   Well. I guess I'm a bit surprised at the cautionary nature of this conversation.

WESTRAY   Good word, cautionary. In Scots Law it defines an instrument in which one person stands as surety for another.

COUNSELOR   As surety.

WESTRAY   Yes.

COUNSELOR   Sounds a bit primitive.

WESTRAY   It is. The problem of course is what happens when the surety turns out to be the more attractive holding.

COUNSELOR   *(Pause)* What about you?

WESTRAY   I can vanish. In a heartbeat. With my money. Can you?

The counselor sits looking out across the room.

WESTRAY   Look, Counselor. The truth is I can walk away from all of this. And I mean all. I know you probably wont believe this but I'll tell you anyway. I think about my life. What have I ever done for the hapless, the hopeless, the horse-fucked? And I'm pretty skeptical about the goodness of the good. I think that if you ransacked the archives of the redeemed you would uncover tales of moral squalor quite beyond the merely appalling. I've pretty much seen it all, Counselor. And it's all shit. I could live in a monastery. Scrub the steps. Wash the pots. Maybe do a little gardening. Why not?

COUNSELOR   You're serious.

WESTRAY   Very.

COUNSELOR   Why dont you?

WESTRAY   In a word? Women.

The counselor smiles.

WESTRAY   I know. But time is not going to stop, Counselor. It's forever. And everything that exists will one day vanish. Forever. And it will take with it every explanation of it that was ever contrived. From Newton and Einstein to Homer and Shakespeare and Michelangelo. Every timeless creation. Your art and your poetry and your science are not even composed of smoke. Alles Vergänglich ist nur ein Gleichnis, as Goethe has it. Everything that perishes is but a likeness. That's really Plato on wheels. A likeness of what? Is that true? I dont want your eyes to glaze completely over, Counselor, but what this is coming down to for me is that seizing the day wont quite do it. I wont flesh out the argument but the only thing ultimately worth your concern is the anguish of your fellow passengers on this hellbound train. I have a lot to answer for. I know that. And I may be a motherfucker but I'm not a hypocrite. You have to help Tom Gray up off the barroom floor. It's little enough. But it's not nothing. All right. Are you ready?

Outside the bar.

WESTRAY   Where are you parked?

COUNSELOR   (*Pointing to his Bentley*) That's me over there.

WESTRAY   (*Looking around*) Some neighborhood. You're lucky it's still there. Anyway. You take care now. You hear?

The counselor waves and crosses the street. Westray watches him go.

WESTRAY   Counselor.

The counselor turns.

WESTRAY   You know why Jesus wasnt born in Mexico dont you?

COUNSELOR   No. Why?

WESTRAY   They couldnt find three wise men *or* a virgin.

The counselor shakes his head. He turns to go.

WESTRAY   Counselor.

The counselor stops and turns.

WESTRAY   Here's something else for you to consider. The beheadings and the mutilations? That's just business. You have to keep up appearances. It's not like there's some smoldering rage at the bottom of it. But let's see if we can guess who it is that they *really* want to kill.

COUNSELOR   I dont know. Who?

WESTRAY   You, Counselor. You.

* * * * *

A small and bare conference room for lawyers and their clients at the Texas State Penitentiary for Women. No windows. A table and two chairs. The counselor is standing at the table with his briefcase, going through his documents. The door opens and a guard hands in a woman in prison uniform and closes the door behind her. She is an attractive woman in her early forties.

COUNSELOR   Hey.

RUTH   Did you bring cigarettes?

COUNSELOR   Yeah.

He digs into his briefcase and comes up with a carton of cigarettes and slides them across the table and she sits and starts to open the carton.

COUNSELOR   (*Arranging his files on the table*) I know
             you use those things to trade with but I
             still dont understand what it is that you
             trade for.

RUTH   (*Opening a pack of cigarettes and tapping
             one out*) You dont want to know.

COUNSELOR   They treating you well?

RUTH   Oh yeah. Peachy.

COUNSELOR   You've got a preliminary hearing on
             the seventeenth. What size dress do
             you wear?

RUTH   I wear a seven.

COUNSELOR   What about shoes?

RUTH   Lo mismo.

COUNSELOR   Seven?

RUTH   Yeah.

COUNSELOR   Hat?

RUTH   What?

COUNSELOR   What size hat.

RUTH   Hat? I dont know what size hat. God-
             damn. What do I need a hat for? A hat?
             You're shittin me.

COUNSELOR   Yes.

RUTH   Smart-ass. You had me goin there for
             a minute. *(She lights a cigarette with a
             lighter and looks up and blows smoke.)* You
             goin to get me somethin sexy to wear?

COUNSELOR   No.

RUTH   You'll have me lookin like a fucking
             schoolmarm.

COUNSELOR   How about a business woman?

RUTH   Yeah. Some business.

*She leans back and blows a stream of smoke across the table
and the counselor waves his hand back and forth to waft it
away. He pulls back the chair and sits at the table.*

COUNSELOR   All right.

RUTH   I know you dont think this room is
             bugged but you dont really know that,
             do you?

COUNSELOR   No. Not if you put it that way.

RUTH   I dont know any other way to put it.

COUNSELOR   What was it you wanted to tell me?

RUTH   My kid's in jail.

COUNSELOR   Oh boy. Where?

RUTH   Fort Hancock.

COUNSELOR   Fort Hancock.

RUTH   Yeah.

COUNSELOR   What was he doing in Fort Hancock?

RUTH   He was comin to see me.

COUNSELOR   What's he in jail for?

RUTH   Speeding.

COUNSELOR   Speeding?

RUTH   Yeah.

COUNSELOR   He couldnt pay the fine?

RUTH   No. He had twelve thousand dol-
            lars on him but they took that off of
            him.

COUNSELOR   Where was he going with twelve thou-
            sand dollars?

RUTH   He was comin here. Like I said.

COUNSELOR   How did you find this out?

RUTH   He called.

COUNSELOR   What else is he charged with?

RUTH   I dont know. Some other stuff. Reck-
            less endangerment or whatever. He said
            they just piled that stuff on on account
            of how fast he was goin.

COUNSELOR   How fast was he going?

RUTH   Two o six.

COUNSELOR   Two o six.

RUTH   Yeah.

COUNSELOR   What is that? Two o six? That's not a
            speed.

RUTH   That's what he said. He didnt want to
              tell me.

COUNSELOR   That's a time of day. Or somebody's
              weight. Two o six? Are you telling me
              he was going two hundred and six miles
              an hour? In what?

RUTH   On that Jap bike of his.

COUNSELOR   Jesus.

RUTH   If you could get him his money back
              he could pay off the fine and get out of
              there.

COUNSELOR   Where did he get the money?

RUTH   I dont know.

COUNSELOR   Well. That's the problem.

RUTH   What's the problem?

COUNSELOR   If you have more than ten thousand
              dollars on you it belongs to the United
              States Government.

RUTH   How is that?

69

COUNSELOR   Because they say so. If you cant explain
              where you got it they take it. You
              might think you should get to keep
              everything up *to* ten grand and the gov-
              ernment would just get the overage but
              the government doesnt think like that.

RUTH   He aint gettin his money back.

COUNSELOR   No.

RUTH   Well I dont see how you can just take
              somebody's money.

COUNSELOR   Yeah, well. Welcome to America. How
              much is the fine?

RUTH   Four hundred dollars.

COUNSELOR   Jesus.

RUTH   I dont guess you'd spring for it, would
              you?

COUNSELOR   Christ. Four hundred dollars?

RUTH   Yes.

COUNSELOR   All right.

RUTH   All right what?

COUNSELOR	All right I'll get him out.
RUTH	You will?
COUNSELOR	Yeah.
RUTH	Really?
COUNSELOR	Yes really.
RUTH	Thanks. I owe you.
COUNSELOR	Yes you do.
RUTH	How about a blowjob?
COUNSELOR	Well, you'd still owe me three eighty.
RUTH	Damn but you are a smart-ass.
COUNSELOR	I know. You bring it out in me. Lighten up, Ruthie.
RUTH	Dont call me that. I hate that name. I dont even like Ruth.

* * * * *

An inspection station on Interstate 10. Vehicles of various sorts are inching along. The border patrol agent waves several cars past and stops a truck and talks to the driver and then

Of course I remember. What I said was: Here, let me help you off with your damp things. And then I pulled down your panties.

Yes.

Ooh.

Oh my goodness.

Is this phone sex?

I know.

Life is being in bed with you. Everything else is just waiting.

Yes.

I love you very much.

Yes.

You too.

Good night.

He lowers the phone into his lap and leans his head back in the chair with his eyes closed.

*****

Reiner and the counselor in an empty nightclub. Late after-noon.

REINER   You see a place like this in the cold light of day it looks pretty seedy. Everything's lighting, really. Lighting and music. You get the right lighting in here and some music and some goodlooking girls and suddenly it's a whole other world.

COUNSELOR   How soon do you think?

REINER   Two weeks. Three, max.

COUNSELOR   You're keeping the dancefloor.

REINER   Yeah. A dancefloor takes up a lot of space but when you have live music and dancing you have a very different sort of place. The door fees dont really amount to all that much but you can charge more for the drinks. But mostly it's just a different milieu. You try and chat up a girl at a bar? That's a no-man's land. How many guys are good at that? But you ask a chick to dance, well, she doesnt want to look like a bitch. You got a better shot. Sitting at the bar she's supposed to tell you to fuck off. You know Peterson, right?

COUNSELOR   Sure.

REINER   Did you know he speaks portuguese?

COUNSELOR   I didnt know that.

REINER   His mother was from Brazil. She grew up here but her whole family's from Brazil. So this cousin of Peterson's shows up and he speaks about three words of english. If that. This is maybe three years ago. We're all out here on Saturday night and the cousin is asking Peterson how do you say may I have this dance, only we get wind of it and we shut Peterson up and we're coaching the cousin on how you say it. Repeat after me: I. want. to. eat. your. pussy. And we work with him till he's pretty much got it down. I vant to ate you poossy. And we send him off. He's this kind of elegant looking guy anyway. He's wearing a suit and everything. And he goes off across the room and he picks out this really great looking girl and he stands in front of her and gives her this little bow and he says: I vant to ate you poossy. Well. The table gets pretty quiet and this girl looks up at him and she says: What did you say? So of course he says it again. Little bow. I vant to ate you poossy. So she studies him for a minute and then she leans over to see past him and of course here's these three guys across the room all hugging each other and just weeping with merriment and she gets up and she takes Peterson's cousin by the hand and she says something like: Well Buster, this is your lucky night. And she takes him out to this Mercedes van in the parking lot and proceeds to fuck his brains out. He's gone for an hour. We dont know *what* the hell is going on. But everything he's ever heard about American girls is true. Finally she leads him back in and she gives him this big sexy kiss and she cuts her eyes over at us to make sure we're watching and she sends him back to the table. Well. We're going nuts. Peterson is trying to get the story out of him and he's jabbering away and rolling his eyes and we're like, what's he saying? what's he saying? And finally it all comes out. And we're just fucking flabbergasted. No way is this guy lying. We look at the girl across the dance floor and she blows us this big kiss. Jesus. We're just fucking stunned. We want all the details of course and fucking Peterson is feeding it to us in driblets. And of course it's the whole thing. Blowjob. The works. Until we're just sitting there staring at each other. And after a while Peterson gets up and he looks at us and he says: I'm going for it. And off he goes. He crosses the floor to this other table where this really cool looking girl is sitting by herself and he gives her the little bow and announces that he vants to ate her poossy. Well of course about this time the husband is coming out of the mens room and he's about eleven feet tall and he looms up behind Peterson and the girl says: Why dont you tell him what you just told me? Anyway, to make a long story short, this guy hits Peterson so hard that he goes completely across the dancefloor on his back with his arms at his sides and comes up against the wall with his head under a chair and just lies there. Apparently dead. This guy hit him so hard that he came out of his loafers. His loafers are still standing at the table. Peterson is lying dead on the dancefloor in his sockfeet with his head under a chair. Now I know what you're thinking. The guy grabs his wife, throws some money on the table, and they split. Right? Not a bit of it. He sits down and snaps his fingers and they order fresh drinks. Like this is every day for him. Anyway they call an ambulance and they haul Peterson off to the hospital and he's got a concussion and a broken jaw. And his loafers are still at the table.

COUNSELOR   Jesus. What happened with you guys?

REINER   Nothing. We left. We'd had enough fun for one evening. Somebody wanted to go over and get Peterson's loafers but I didnt think that was such a good idea. Anyway. The other big space-eater is the bandstand. They just had a jukebox in here. I think what I'm going to do is take that wall out and get rid of the hallway.

* * * * *

Yard of the Pump Masters Septic Tank Pumping Company. Early morning. The trucks are pulling out one by one and the yard master is checking them off on his clipboard. When they are all gone there is one truck left in the yard.

* * * * *

A large motorcycle store in the city. A man enters and stands looking. He crosses to where a Kawasaki ZX-12 motorcycle is mounted and circling slowly on a motorized dais. The dais is marked off with a blue felt rope and the man approaches and stands looking at the bike for a moment, then unhooks the rope and lets it fall to the floor and mounts the dais and stands circling with it. A clerk talking to a customer nearby sees him.

BIKE CLERK   Excuse me a minute.

The clerk comes over to the dais. The man has taken a steel tape measure from his coat pocket and is measuring the height of the Kawasaki at the handlebars.

BIKE CLERK   Sir, may I help you?

WIRE-MAN   *(Looking at the bike while the steel tape spools up and clicks home. He pops his lips.)* Nope. I'm all done.

The man steps down from the revolving dais and puts the tape measure back in his coat pocket and goes past the clerk toward the door. The clerk bends and picks up the rope and hooks the end of it back in the stand and turns and watches the man as he leaves.

*   *   *   *   *

Church, interior. Five women are standing in line along the rear wall of the church waiting to go to confession.

The women are both hispanic and anglo. At the front of the line is Malkina, dressed casually but fashionably. The woman in the confessional pushes back the curtain and exits with her head bowed and Malkina enters the confessional booth.

MALKINA   Hi.

PRIEST   Hi?

MALKINA   Oh. Bless me father for I have sinned.

Silence.

PRIEST   How long has it been since your last confession?

MALKINA   I've never been before. This is my first.

PRIEST   Are you Catholic?

MALKINA   No.

PRIEST   Why are you here?

MALKINA   I wanted to confess my sins.

PRIEST   Have you ever done this before?

MALKINA   No. I told you.

PRIEST	I couldnt give you absolution. Even if you did. Confess. You couldnt be forgiven.
MALKINA	I know. I just wanted to tell someone what I'd done and I thought why not go to a professional.
PRIEST	Have you thought about taking instructions?
MALKINA	That's not something I do very well.
PRIEST	I mean in order to become a Catholic. You take what are called instructions. You learn about the faith. What it means. Then you could confess and you would be forgiven for your sins.
MALKINA	How do you know?
PRIEST	Excuse me?
MALKINA	What if they're unforgivable?
PRIEST	Nothing is unforgivable.
MALKINA	Yeah? What's the worst thing anyone ever told you?

PRIEST	I wouldnt be at liberty to tell you a thing like that. The priest can never reveal anything from the confessional.
MALKINA	That bad, huh? Well, I havent killed anybody. But I've been pretty bad. I think. I dont really know because I'm not all that sure about the rules.
PRIEST	Where are you from?
MALKINA	Buenos Aires. You?
PRIEST	Excuse me?
MALKINA	Where are you from?
PRIEST	Phoenix. Arizona.
MALKINA	I know where Phoenix is. Do you ever go out on dates with girls?
PRIEST	No. Of course not.
MALKINA	Boys?
PRIEST	No. What did you want to tell me.
MALKINA	What if I'd done something really bad? What if I had killed somebody. Would you call the police?

PRIEST   No.

MALKINA   I killed somebody.

PRIEST   You said that you hadnt. Look, I'm
              sorry, but we have people here waiting
              to go to confession.

MALKINA   They can wait. I did. You want to
              throw me out because I'm not a Catho-
              lic but what if I'd said I was one? I
              mean, you dont carry a card around do
              you?

PRIEST   Who did you talk to about this?

MALKINA   Why did I talk to somebody?

PRIEST   You said Bless me father.

MALKINA   I asked a friend. But she didnt know I
              was going to do it. I asked her if non-
              Catholics could go to confession but
              she said no you couldnt.

PRIEST   But you didnt believe her.

MALKINA   No. I believed her. I just wanted to see
              what would happen.

PRIEST   So are we done here then?

MALKINA	I havent told you my sins yet.
PRIEST	I dont want to hear your sins. There would be no point. Are you baptized?
MALKINA	I dont know. It's possible.
PRIEST	Your parents never told you?
MALKINA	I never knew my parents. They were thrown out of a helicopter into the Atlantic Ocean when I was three. Look, you dont have to do the forgiveness thing. All you would have to do is listen. To the sins. You could even pretend I was lying. If you didnt like what you were hearing.
PRIEST	Why would you lie?
MALKINA	I wouldnt. But you could think that I was. Maybe I wanted to be wicked but I didnt have the stones for it. So I would just make up stuff. Women tell you about sex, dont they?
PRIEST	I cant talk about that.
MALKINA	Yes. But every woman who comes to confess tells you that she is an adulterer or a fornicator or something or else why

would she be here? The only women who dont come are the ones who arent doing anything. So you must get an unusual picture of women. You must think that they are just having sex all the time. That that's all they do. Anyway, I think that women might make up sexy things to tell you just to make you crazy. Dont you think that's possible?

PRIEST   No.

MALKINA   But you dont know. Suppose I told you that I had sex with my sister. Would you believe that?

PRIEST   You really have to go now.

MALKINA   Because I did. We did it every night. As soon as the lights were out we were at it. We'd be falling asleep at our desks the next day at school. They didnt know what was wrong with us. But that's not the worst thing. Where are you going?

The priest pushes back the curtain and exits the confessional. Malkina, kneeling, turns and pushes aside the curtain. The priest is hurrying up the aisle, blessing himself.

MALKINA   *(Standing up and calling to the priest)* Wait! I wasnt finished!

The women waiting to go to the confession are confused, horrified. One of them blesses herself.

* * * * *

Border city. Evening. An outdoor cafe adjoining a parking lot. Metal chairs and tables. Traffic. A Mexican man is sitting at one of the tables with a cup of coffee before him and a newspaper. The young man in green pulls up on the Kawasaki ZX-12. He takes off the gloves and the helmet and puts the gloves inside the helmet and steps off of the bike and walks down to where the man is sitting and kicks back a chair and sits down.

A man and a girl are sitting in a parked car. The girl is watching the table through a pair of binoculars.

GIRL   I wont be able to get what the kid is saying. Is that okay?

MAN (JAIME)   We dont care what the kid is saying.

She is watching through the binoculars and writing on a pad on a clipboard.

The man at the table rises and leaves, leaving the paper on the table. The kid sits at the table and opens the newspaper and sits reading.

JAIME   Did you get it?

GIRL	Yeah. It's not much.
JAIME	That's okay. Keep your eye on him.
GIRL	I am.
JAIME	This guy doesnt read the fucking news-papers.
GIRL	I know.

The kid rakes an object from under the paper into his helmet and puts down the paper and stands and puts the helmet under his arm and crosses the plaza to his bike and puts his foot over the bike and starts it with the starter and pulls his gloves from the helmet and lays them on the tank in front of him and pulls on the helmet and fastens the strap and then pulls on the gloves and kicks back the stand and pulls away into the traffic.

JAIME	Could you see what it was?
GIRL	No. But it's in the helmet.
JAIME	Yeah. It's in the helmet.

The man is dialing a number on his cell phone.

* * * * *

Reiner's house. Malkina is on the phone.

MALKINA   Look Jaime, he doesnt have to know, he just has to do what I tell him to do. No. It's already downloaded. It's programmed to pick up the bike at above five thousand rpm's and that is coded into the global. The only way we can lose him is if he suddenly decides not to drive over thirty miles an hour and I'll leave you to think about how likely that is. Call me in an hour.

Jaime and the girl in the parked car. Jaime clicks off the cell phone and looks at the girl.

JAIME   Let's go.

* * * * *

Corner table in an upscale club. The counselor and Reiner.

REINER   I dont know. Women have funny ideas about sex. They're supposed to be so modest? Let me tell you. When they get it into their head that they want to fuck they're like a freight train. The things I've learned about women? Fuck. About half of it I'd like to forget.

He takes a sip of his drink.

COUNSELOR   I'm not sure I follow you. What is it
            you'd like to forget? For instance.

REINER   You dont want to know.

COUNSELOR   Sure I do.

REINER   Not the worst things.

COUNSELOR   Those in particular.

REINER   Not the very worst.

COUNSELOR   Come off it, Reiner.

REINER   I dont know. Let's talk about something
            else.

COUNSELOR   Are you shitting me? What else?

REINER   Yeah. I dont know. I shouldnt tell you
            this.

COUNSELOR   Just pull up your socks and tell me.
            What is it you'd like to forget?

REINER   All right. I'd like to forget about Mal-
            kina fucking my car.

COUNSELOR   What?

REINER	See?
COUNSELOR	What did you just say?
REINER	I said I'd like to forget about Malkina fucking my car. I think.
COUNSELOR	What the hell are you talking about?
REINER	You remember the 328 I had.
COUNSELOR	Sure. Nice car.
REINER	Very nice car. Not a V-12 but a better car than the 308. Which was an embarrassment for a Ferrari. Westray had one and he said that it wouldnt pull a greasy string out of a cat's ass. His metaphor. Is that a metaphor? Anyway, this was a while back. Not that long. We'd been getting it on for a while and we came back one night—we were staying up at Cloudcroft. Mostly for that great stretch of road between Cloudcroft and Ruidoso. And we drove out on the golf course and parked and we're sitting there talking and for no particular reason that I could see she lifts herself up and slides off her knickers and hands them to me and gets out of the car. I

asked her what she was doing and she says: I'm going to fuck your car. Jesus. She tells me to leave the door open. Turns out she wants the domelight on. So she goes around and climbs up on the hood of the Ferrari and pulls her dress up around her waist and spreads herself across the windshield in front of me with no panties on. And she's had this Brazilian wax job. And she begins to rub herself on the glass. Dont even think I'm making this up. You cant make this up. I mean, she was a dancer, right? In Argentina? She danced at the opera thing down there. I've seen the clippings. And she does this full split and starts rubbing herself up and down on the glass and she's lying on the roof of the car and she leans down over the side to see if I'm watching. Like, no, I'm sitting there reading my e-mail. And she gestures at me to crank down the window and she leans in and kisses me. Upside down. And then she tells me that she's going to come. And I thought, well, I'm losing my fucking mind. That's what's happening here. It was like one of those catfish things. One of those bottom feeders you see going up the side of the aquarium. Sucking its way up the glass? It was just. I dont know. It was just . . . Hallucinatory. You see a thing like that, it changes you.

COUNSELOR   Jesus.

REINER   Tell me about it.

COUNSELOR   Did she?

REINER   Did she what?

COUNSELOR   Did she come?

REINER   Yeah. Sure. Then she just laid there. Spread out across the windshield. Finally she climbs down and comes around and gets in the car and shuts the door and I hand her her knickers and she puts them in her purse and she sort of looks at me. Like to see what I thought about that. What I thought about that? Jesus. I dont know what I thought about that. I still dont. It was too gynecological to be sexy. Almost. But mostly I was just fucking stunned. Maybe I was thinking about the leather. I dont know.

COUNSELOR   The leather.

REINER   Yeah. The seats. You know. Where she
              was sitting? I mean the car is about two
              weeks old. Finally I asked her if she'd
              ever done that before and she said she'd
              done everything before. Of course. So
              I start the engine and turn on the lights
              but the windshield is all smeared and I
              didnt have anything to wipe it with and
              of course she suggested that I get out
              and lick it off and I tried the wipers but
              naturally the windshield washer thing
              doesnt work because the Italians dont
              really believe in that sort of thing and
              finally I took off my socks and got out
              of the car and used them.

COUNSELOR   Catfish?

REINER   I dont know. Yeah. I think so.

COUNSELOR   Do you think she knew the kind of
              effect this might have on a guy?

REINER   Jesus, Counselor. Are you kidding? She
              knows everything.

COUNSELOR   You dont think this is an odd thing to
              tell me?

REINER   I think it's an odd thing.

COUNSELOR Yes, but I mean why would you tell me this? I mean, I know this woman. Why is it okay to tell a thing like that about somebody . . .

REINER Somebody I'm banging?

COUNSELOR Come on, Reiner.

REINER I dont know. You're probably right. Maybe I wanted to see what you'd say. Maybe there's more to it than that. Maybe I'm scared.

COUNSELOR You're scared?

REINER Yeah. Probably. Yeah. Sometimes she scares the shit out of me.

COUNSELOR Because of that?

REINER No. Not that.

COUNSELOR You're in love with her.

REINER I dont know what I am. Yeah. I suppose I am in love with her. You dont think that's cause for worry? It's like being in love with . . . what? Easeful death? Fuck it. Fuck it, Counselor. Just forget the whole thing.

COUNSELOR   It's just that I dont know what it is that
             you're trying to tell me.

REINER   I know.

COUNSELOR   Does this have anything to do with the
             deal?

REINER   I dont know. You're right. I shouldnt
             have told you. Just forget it.

COUNSELOR   Forget it.

REINER   Yeah.

COUNSELOR   How do you propose that I do that?

REINER   I dont know. Jesus, Counselor. How do
             I know?

                    *   *   *   *   *

*Malkina's bedroom. She sits in a robe in front of the fire. The
cheetahs are lying on the rug at her feet. She is listening on
the phone.*

LAURA   No. I had a dream about you. And when
             I woke up I couldnt remember why the
             dream was so troubling even though I
             could still remember the dream. I just

wanted to call and see if you were all right.

MALKINA   Are you superstitious?

LAURA   I dont think so. No more than the next person.

MALKINA   And who would that be?

LAURA   Excuse me?

MALKINA   The next person. You're not gay are you?

LAURA   No. Of course not. I shouldnt have called. I know you think my world naive. But is that so bad?

MALKINA   I dont know. I cant advise you.

LAURA   I know.

MALKINA   You should be careful what you wish for, Angel. You might not get it.

LAURA   I know.

MALKINA   Do you?

LAURA   Yes. I do.

MALKINA   Good. I'll see you at the club.

* * * * *

*Two-lane blacktop road through the high desert. Night. A car
passes and the lights recede down the long straight and fade
out. A man walks out from the scrub cedars that line the road
and stands in the middle of the road and lights a cigarette.
He is carrying a roll of thin monel wire over one shoulder. He continues across the road to the fence. A tall metal
pipe is mounted to one of the fenceposts and at the top—some
twenty feet off the ground—is a floodlight. The man pushes
the button on a small plastic sending unit and the light comes
on, flooding the road and the man's face. He turns it off and
walks down the fence line a good hundred yards to the corner
of the fence and here he drops the coil of wire to the ground
and takes a flashlight from his back pocket and puts it in his
teeth and takes a pair of leather gloves from his belt and puts
them on. Then he loops the wire around the corner post and
pulls the end of the wire through the loop and wraps it about
six times around the wire itself and tucks the end several
times inside the loop and then takes the wire in both hands
and hauls it as tight as he can get it. Then he takes the coil of
wire and walks out and crosses the road, letting out the wire
behind him. In the cedars on the far side a flatbed truck is
parked with the bed of the truck facing the road. He walks up
to the rear of the truck and turns and pulls the wire taut and
shines his flashlight back along the length of it. There is an
iron pipe at the right rear of the truckbed mounted vertically*

in a pair of collars so that it can slide up and down and the man threads the wire through a hole in the pipe and pulls it taut and stops it from sliding back by clamping the wire with a pair of visegrips. Then he walks back out to the road and takes a tape measure from his belt and measures the height of the wire from the road surface. He goes back to the truck and lowers the iron pipe in its collars and clamps it in place again with a threaded lever that he turns by hand against the vertical rod. He goes out to the road and measures the wire again and comes back and wraps the end of the wire through a heavy three-inch iron ring and walks to the front of the truck where he pulls the wire taut and wraps it around itself to secure the ring at the end of the wire and then pulls the ring over a hook mounted in the side rail of the truck bed. He stands looking at it. He strums the wire with his fingers. It gives off a deep resonant note. He unhooks the ring and walks the wire to the rear of the truck until it lies slack on the ground and in the road. He lays the ring on the truck bed and goes around and he takes a walkie-talkie from a work-bag in the cab of the truck and stands in the open door of the truck listening. He checks his watch by the domelight in the cab.

WIRE-MAN   Anything?

VOICE (MALE)   He's coming.

WIRE-MAN   You're at eight miles.

VOICE   Yeah.

WIRE-MAN   That's less than three minutes.

VOICE	Yeah. Flat out it's about two minutes and twenty seconds.
WIRE-MAN	Can you hear him?
VOICE	Not yet.

They wait.

VOICE	There he is.
WIRE-MAN	Yeah. I hear him. All right. Let's do it.

He hangs up the walkie-talkie and takes the cigarette from his mouth and grinds it into the dirt and shuts the door of the truck. He looks at his watch. Very thin in the distance we can hear the highpitched scream of the Kawasaki bike flat out at eleven thousand rpm.

Shot of the green rider bent low over the bike at one hundred and ninety miles an hour. Suddenly the floodlight comes on and he raises up and turns his head to look at it.

The truck. The desert is suddenly lit to the north of the wire-man and he takes the ring and carries it forward and pulls it over the hook. The wire hums.

Shot of green rider with his face turned back to the flood-light now behind him. Suddenly his head zips away and in the helmet it goes bouncing down the highway behind the bike. The bike continues on, the motor slows and dies to silence, and in the distance we see a long slither of sparks recede into the dark.

The truck. The man clips the wire at the ring with a pair of wirecutters and the wire zips away. He walks out to the road with the walkie-talkie. In the road he shines the light down the blacktop and then walks down the roadside ditch until he comes to the helmet.

WIRE-MAN   *(Into walkie-talkie)* We're good. Yeah. Over and out.

He puts away the walkie-talkie and bends over and picks up the helmet. It is surprisingly heavy. He goes back to the truck and opens the cab door on the driver's side and puts the helmet in the floor and shuts the door and goes out to the road and crosses to the fence where he cuts the wire free from the fence-post and begins to wind it up as he walks, passing the wire over his elbow at each turn to make a coil of the wire. At the truck he stows the wire in a toolbox under the bed of the truck and gets in the truck and starts it and turns on the lights and turns out into the road.

Desert. Night. At the fence the man is disassembling the pole and floodlight. Disconnecting the wires. The pole is made of sections of 1-5/8 inch galvanized chainlink fencepost that slide one into the next and he puts these in the bed of the truck and puts the small components in the under-bed toolbox.

Desert. Night. The truck pulls out and drives past the head-less body sprawled in the road. Then it stops. The man looks out the window of the truck back at the body, then backs up the truck and gets out. He picks up the feet and drags the body into the ditch and wipes his hands on his pants and then gets back in the truck and pulls away down the highway.

* * * * *

Death row cell, Texas State Penitentiary. Night. Ruth wakes and lies looking up at the ceiling. She sits up, pushing back the bed covers. She sits on the edge of the bunk with her hands folded.

* * * * *

Front gate of the septic-tank company. The flatbed truck pulls up and the wire-man gets out and shuts the door. He is holding a battery-driven diegrinder in one hand and he watches the road behind him where a single light is approaching. Sound of a motorcycle. The cycle pulls up and halts and the rider gets off and kicks down the stand and the wire-man goes to the gate and turns on the diegrinder and bends to cut the padlock on the gate. A sheaf of sparks lights up the area and the lock falls to the ground in about twenty seconds. He pushes open the gate and then bends and picks up the lock and juggles it in his hand and throws it into the bushes.

WIRE-MAN   *(Shaking his hand)* Hot son of a bitch.

The second man goes past and turns on a flashlight.

SECOND MAN You know which one it is?

WIRE-MAN   Yeah. It's got Arizona plates.

The wire-man goes back to the flatbed truck and opens the passenger side door and takes the green motorcycle helmet off the seat and takes out of the helmet a set of keys and a computerized jumper cable with three color coded jacks and shuts the door and follows the second man into the yard where the septic-tank trucks are parked. The second man has opened the door of the truck and pulled the hood release and he goes around to the front of the truck and opens the hood.

WIRE-MAN   Let me see your light.

He takes the light and goes along the side of the truck and picks up a loose set of wires.

SECOND MAN You know how it goes?

WIRE-MAN   Yeah. It's color coded. Red to red, green to green. Black to black. Here. Hold the light.

He plugs in the connections and hands the keys to the second man.

WIRE-MAN   See if it'll start.

The second man gets in the truck and turns the key. He turns it again.

WIRE-MAN   Wait a minute. This thing's got a switch
                on it. How do you say *on* in Mexican?

SECOND MAN   You're shittin me.

WIRE-MAN   Try it now.

The second man cranks the engine and it starts. Wire-man drops the hood and steps back.

* * * * *

The counselor is sitting in his chair in his condo, listening to Westray on the telephone.

WESTRAY   Counselor.

COUNSELOR   Que pasó?

WESTRAY   We've got a problem.

Silence.

WESTRAY   You there?

COUNSELOR   I'm here. How bad a problem?

WESTRAY   Let's say pretty bad. Then multiply by
               ten.

COUNSELOR   Fuck.

WESTRAY   What time can you meet me tomor-
               row?

COUNSELOR   It is tomorrow.

WESTRAY   What time?

COUNSELOR   Nine oclock.

WESTRAY   All right. Where.

COUNSELOR   How about the coffeeshop at the Coro-
               nado.

WESTRAY   How about McDonald's? We can start
               getting used to our new lifestyle.

COUNSELOR   (Softly) Jesus. Coronado. Nine oclock.

WESTRAY   See you at nine.

*The counselor hangs up the phone and leans back and puts his
hand over his eyes.*

COUNSELOR   Fuck. Fuckety fuck fuck fuck fuck.

Coffeeshop of an elegant downtown hotel. The counselor is seated at a corner table watching Westray enter and scan the room. Westray is dressed in a goodlooking suit, no tie. Carrying a newspaper. The counselor looks at his watch. Westray crosses the room to the table.

WESTRAY   Morning.

COUNSELOR   Good morning.

Westray lays the paper on the table and sits.

WESTRAY   You seen the paper?

COUNSELOR   No.

The waitress puts down menus and glasses of water. She knows the counselor and flirts a bit with him. They wait till she has gone before they talk again.

WESTRAY   Do you know who the Green Hornet is?

COUNSELOR   The Green Hornet.

WESTRAY   Yes.

COUNSELOR   He's a cartoon character.

WESTRAY   It's all right. The newspaper doesnt know either. He's a biker.

COUNSELOR   Shit. *(Leaning back)* All right. What? Is he in custody?

WESTRAY   In a manner of speaking, yes.

The counselor reaches for the paper.

COUNSELOR   It's in the paper? What has he done?

WESTRAY   You dont know anything about this.

COUNSELOR   *(Thumbing through the paper)* About what?

The counselor stops and looks at Westray.

COUNSELOR   What?

Westray holds out his hand in a gesture that says: Go ahead.

WESTRAY   Like I said: They dont even know who he is.

COUNSELOR   He had no ID on him.

WESTRAY   No. No ID. And no head, actually.

COUNSELOR   No head?

WESTRAY   Mmm.

The counselor sits reading. He looks up.

COUNSELOR   What the hell is this? Does his mother
               know?

WESTRAY   Oh yes. She thinks they'll probably get
               to her before the State does. Anyway
               they did find his head. Read on. Read
               the part where it says it appeared to
               have been thrown from the window of
               a car at speed. I sort of liked that. Car
               at speed.

COUNSELOR   *(Reading)* Mother of God. *(Looking up)*
               A police spokesperson said the matter is
               under further investigation?

WESTRAY   I hope you havent done something stu-
               pid.

COUNSELOR   *(Pushing the paper aside)* All right. Why
               dont you tell me what this is about.

WESTRAY   I thought you might be able to tell me.
               I had a call from our business partners.
               They wanted to talk with you.

COUNSELOR   Do I want to talk to them?

WESTRAY   I dont think so. In these circles talk has
             a slightly different meaning. Anyway,
             it seems that the deceased was working
             for them. Now the shipment is missing
             and the only thing they have to go on is
             that he was a client of yours.

COUNSELOR   Client? He wasnt a client. I paid a
             speeding ticket for him.

WESTRAY   Well. I'm perfectly willing to believe
             you had nothing to do with this but I'm
             not the party you have to convince.

COUNSELOR   Convince of what, for Christ sake?

WESTRAY   That this is just some sort of coinci-
             dence. Because they dont really believe
             in coincidences. They've heard of them.
             They've just never seen one.

COUNSELOR   God. So what happened to the ship-
             ment?

WESTRAY   I asked them that.

COUNSELOR   And?

WESTRAY   They said: Se fue.

COUNSELOR   Se fue? Jesus.

WESTRAY   Mmm.

COUNSELOR   I need to call his mother.

WESTRAY   Probably not such a good idea.

COUNSELOR   Why is that?

WESTRAY   She says she's going to have you killed.

COUNSELOR   Sweet Jesus.

The waitress comes to the table.

WAITRESS   Sorry about that. What can I get you to
               drink?

COUNSELOR   Hemlock.

WAITRESS   I'm sorry?

WESTRAY   I'd like an orange juice and coffee and
               he's having a double Maalox with a side
               of Oxycontin.

*The waitress looks from one to the other, tapping her pencil
on her order pad.*

WESTRAY   Sorry. Just bring us two coffees. And
               my OJ.

The waitress moves away.

WESTRAY   How did you wind up with her?

COUNSELOR   The mother?

WESTRAY   The mother. The mother of all mothers.

COUNSELOR   It was a court appointment. An appeal. One of Ferguson's fucked up deals. Look. They cant hook me up to this. What do they think I would *do* with the stuff?

WESTRAY   They dont know. They dont care. They assume that everybody knows somebody. They do. You need to think about this, Counselor. These people are out twenty mil. Do you know how serious that is?

The counselor sits back and studies Westray.

COUNSELOR   They think we're all involved.

WESTRAY   Why wouldnt they?

COUNSELOR   Reiner too.

WESTRAY   Yes. You fucking genius.

COUNSELOR   *(Looking away)* Jesus.

The waitress returns and sets down their coffee and the juice.

WAITRESS   Did you want to order?

WESTRAY   No thanks. We've sort of lost our appetites.

COUNSELOR   This is fine, Alexis.

The waitress moves away.

WESTRAY   Have you ever seen a snuff film?

COUNSELOR   No. Have you?

WESTRAY   No. Would you?

COUNSELOR   I would not.

WESTRAY   Because the consumer of the product is essential to its production. You cant watch without being implicated in a murder.

COUNSELOR   But you know someone who's seen one.

WESTRAY   I do. He said that the girl was beheaded with a machete. She was about fourteen and she was being sodomized by a hooded figure and looking into the camera and crying when her head fell off.

COUNSELOR   Jesus.

WESTRAY   You might want to think about that the next time you do a line.

COUNSELOR   I dont do drugs.

WESTRAY   I'm glad to hear that, Counselor. Because it's what was done to her next that you really wouldnt want to see. I wont ask you to use your imagination because I sincerely hope that it wouldnt be up to the task. They led forth a portly and slightly older fellow naked and erect and wearing like the others a black hood with eyeholes. To address himself to the naked and quivering and headless corpse in all its gushing menses which you must remember would not have served his purpose had she not been young and pretty. And all of this he has paid for. Now. What do you think it cost? Ballpark.

The counselor sits with a blank face. Then suddenly he gri-maces and turns his face away.

COUNSELOR   Oh Jesus.

WESTRAY   Mmm.

COUNSELOR   God. Do you think that's true?

WESTRAY   I know it's true.

COUNSELOR   There cant be such people.

WESTRAY   Think again, Counselor.

COUNSELOR   Good God.

WESTRAY   The point, Counselor, is that you may think that there are things that these people are incapable of. There aren't.

The counselor sits staring at the table. Westray sips his coffee. The counselor raises his head and looks at him.

WESTRAY   It's always later than you think, Coun-selor. I should have jumped ship a long time ago and I didn't.

COUNSELOR   What are you going to do?

WESTRAY   Me? I'll be gone in no time at all.

COUNSELOR   Where will you go?

WESTRAY   Yeah, right.

COUNSELOR   You think I'd rat you out.

WESTRAY   Counselor, if these people got hold of her the Virgin Mary would rat you out.

COUNSELOR   Jesus.

WESTRAY   I've known this was coming for a long time. For all my sins I still believe in a moral order. I'm not so sure about you. And it's not that you're going down, Counselor. It's what you're taking down with you. All right. Take care.

He rises and leaves.

* * * * *

An upscale restaurant.

MALKINA   So where do you think this is going, mi Capitan.

REINER   This?

MALKINA   Yes.

REINER   I cant really take your question seriously. It's going where it's going.

MALKINA   Either you think everything is going to be okay or you dont want to think about it at all.

REINER   Because the third possibility is not something you're ready to admit to.

MALKINA   Yes. The excluded middle. The Tertium non Datur.

REINER   I dont know, Baby Girl. You read that stuff, I dont. *(Pause)* I dont like decisions made for me. But if you put them off, waiting for the maximum information, that might be what happens. You think that there is still space enough to make the decision. And then there isnt.

MALKINA   Space.

REINER   Yes.

MALKINA   Greed always takes you to the edge, doesnt it?

REINER   That's not what greed does. That's what greed is.

MALKINA	You know that when the axe comes through the door I'll already be gone. Dont you.
REINER	That's fair enough.
MALKINA	I'm not entirely faithless. You'll see.

Reiner smiles.

MALKINA	You're in trouble.
REINER	Probably.
MALKINA	What do you want me to tell you?
REINER	I dont know. What do you?
MALKINA	I dont know. I miss the ladies.

Reiner tilts his head. Almost a shrug.

MALKINA	I dont know what I can tell you.
REINER	About the ladies?
MALKINA	No. Not about that.
REINER	You'll figure it out.

MALKINA   I know. But the space is closing fast. I
            know that. The space that you spoke
            of.

REINER   I dont want to lose you. There.

MALKINA   I know.

REINER   Are you hungry?

MALKINA   I'm starving.

                    *   *   *   *   *

*Reiner's office. The counselor is pacing up and back. He stops
and turns.*

COUNSELOR   You talked to him.

REINER   Yeah. I talked to him.

COUNSELOR   Can we go somewhere?

REINER   *(Rising)* Sure.

COUNSELOR   I dont feel comfortable in here.

REINER   Come on.

                    *   *   *   *   *

Booth in a coffeeshop.

REINER   You asked me that.

COUNSELOR   Yeah. But you didnt answer that.

REINER   You think I know something you dont. Maybe I think the same thing.

COUNSELOR   I've told you everything I know.

REINER   What are you going to do?

COUNSELOR   I dont know. What are you?

REINER   I dont know.

COUNSELOR   That's what Westray said. But he did know. Didnt he?

REINER   I know you dont have any money or you wouldnt be in this jackpot in the first place.

COUNSELOR   Maybe.

REINER   Yeah. Well. I know why I'm in it. Do you?

COUNSELOR   Sure. Same as you. Greed.

REINER   I dont think so. You got in trouble. I
            tried to appeal to your greed two years
            ago. No deal. Now it's too late. Greed
            is greatly overrated. But fear isnt.

COUNSELOR   What do you think I should do?

REINER   I dont know, Counselor. They know
            that you're stupid. They just dont know
            how stupid.

COUNSELOR   You say that like it's my hole card.

REINER   Maybe it is.

COUNSELOR   Maybe I could talk to them.

REINER   And say what?

COUNSELOR   I'd tell them the truth.

REINER   You're just a fucking wonder. Did you
            know that? Go ahead.

COUNSELOR   Go ahead what?

REINER   With the truth. I'd like to hear it.

COUNSELOR   I'd tell them that I'd never even met this
            kid. That I'd gotten him out of jail on a
            speeding charge.

REINER   Okay. How did he happen to hire you?

COUNSELOR   He didnt. I got him out of jail as a favor
             to his mother.

REINER   Okay. How did you happen to know the
             mother?

COUNSELOR   I was appointed by the court to repre-
             sent her in an appeal on a capital mur-
             der case. She killed her husband. The
             kid's stepfather.

REINER   Did you know what the kid did for a
             living?

COUNSELOR   No.

REINER   But you do now.

COUNSELOR   I do now. Yes.

REINER   And would it please you to tell the court
             what that occupation was?

COUNSELOR   How did I get in court?

REINER   Sorry. I guess I was getting ahead of
             myself.

COUNSELOR   Very funny.

Reiner stirs his coffee. He lays the spoon steaming on the table.

REINER   Yeah. Well. Probably not.

＊ ＊ ＊ ＊ ＊

The counselor is on a busy street downtown. It is raining. He turns into a cafe and approaches a woman sitting at a table with a poodle.

COUNSELOR   Mam, I'm terribly sorry to bother you but my phone is out and it's something of an emergency. Could I use your phone for just a minute?

The woman looks at him and then hands him her phone which is lying on the table. The counselor dials.

COUNSELOR   Where are you?

I cant call you on my phone.

No. You cant.

Go to a hotel and call me later.

Dont go to the apartment.

Just dont.

It's very important.

I've got to go.

Dont call anyone.

No.

Anyone. I love you.

He rings off and hands the woman her phone.

COUNSELOR   Thank you very much. Very kind of you.

He turns and goes out. The woman finishes her coffee and rises with the dog under her arm and goes out. She puts up her red umbrella and stands holding the poodle and looking out at the street in the rain.

* * * * *

The septic-tank truck on a two-lane blacktop road in central Texas. A late-model sedan is following it, two men in the car. The passenger in the sedan plugs a flashing red rooflight into the cigar lighter in the dash and reaches out the window and places the light on the roof of the car. Then he takes a black box off the seat and holds it at the window and turns it on and it begins to emit a police siren sound. The septic-tank truck slows and pulls over onto the verge and comes to a halt. The sedan pulls in some distance behind it and the two men get out, putting on white Stetson hats. They are dressed in boots and tan slacks and white shirts and wear automatic sidearms.

The driver of the truck—wire-man—watches them in the rearview mirror. The boots of the co-driver of the truck are moving back along the passenger side of the truck. The driver starts the truck and pulls away. The two men in the road have almost reached the truck and they draw their pistols and run forward. The co-driver of the truck is now lying in the bar ditch and when the truck clears his position the two men in the road are exposed directly in front of him and he opens fire on them with a pistol, dropping one of them dead in the road and wounding the other in the leg. The wounded man dives into the ditch on the other side of the road. The truck has come to a stop again, angled slightly toward the road, and the driver opens fire on the wounded man with a pistol from the truck window. The wounded man presses himself flat in the ditch and takes careful aim with his pistol and shoots the driver in the head. The driver's pistol clatters into the road. The co-driver in the ditch sees the pistol fall. He studies the far side of the road and then backs down into the ditch and crouches and runs along the ditch toward the truck. The wounded man sees the man's back moving along the ditch and he stands and fires three rounds after him. The last round hits the tank of the truck and brown sewage starts to spout from the hole. The co-driver reaches the truck and opens the door and clambers in over the body slumped in the floor and crouching over the body he reaches and pushes the clutch to the floor with his hand and drops the shifter into first gear and reaches and releases the emergency brake. He pushes down the accelerator with one hand and lets the clutch out with the other and the truck moves forward into the road. The wounded man climbs out of the ditch and hobbles back to the car and gets in and shuts the door. He lays the pistol on the seat and reaches under the seat and takes out an AR-15 machine-pistol and starts the car and pulls out down the road after the truck. The truck has wandered to the far side of the road and the car pulls up along the passenger side of the truck and the wounded man opens fire with the AR-15, emptying the magazine into the door of the truck. Then he slows the car and backs away and pulls to the verge and sits watching. The truck veers slowly off in front of him and rolls down into the bar ditch where it tilts up onto two wheels and balances for a moment and then drops back onto all four wheels and sits there in silence. The man in the car sits watching. In the rearview mirror he can see a car approaching, very small on the long stretch of blacktop road. He can see the pistol lying in the road and beyond that the dead body. He eases the car forward and comes abreast of the truck in the ditch and stops. He looks in the rearview mirror again. The approaching car is shimmering in the heatwaves off the road. The man's trouserleg is dark with blood to his boot. He places his hand on his thigh and leans forward slightly in pain. He turns the AR-15 on the seat and ejects the empty magazine and reaches under the seat and gets hold of a small canvas bag and puts it in his lap and unzips it and takes out a loaded magazine from among the half dozen in the bag and loads the AR-15 and pulls back the slide to chamber a round. The approaching car has slowed. Now it stops. It turns sideways in the road and backs up and swings around and heads back the way it came. The wounded man has opened the door and he steps out and levels the AR-15 and opens fire on the fleeing car. He empties the magazine and then lowers the gun and stands watching. The car slows and drifts off the road and down into the bar ditch and comes to a stop. The man reaches into the car and gets another magazine and reloads the AR-15 and turns and goes down the bank to the truck.

Sewage is still leaking from the bullethole in the tank. The man limps up to the passenger side of the truck with the gun at the ready and pulls open the door and steps back. Then he steps up and reaches into the truck and pulls out a body by the belt and lets it fall into the grass. Then he pulls the other one out on top of it. He turns and climbs up out of the ditch and stands in the road and looks up the road and down. He limps down the road to the car and gets the pistol and the pouch of magazines off the seat and takes the keys from the ignition and goes to the rear of the car and opens the trunk and gets out his bag. He opens the bag and puts in the machine-pistol and the magazines and closes it again. He puts the pistol in his belt at the small of his back and closes the trunk and walks down the road to the body and sets the bag in the road and takes his knife from his pocket and opens it and kneels painfully and cuts open the dead man's rear pocket and takes out the man's billfold and opens his bag and puts the billfold in and shuts the bag and gets to his feet and picks up the bag and goes back up the road toward the truck.

The man is sitting in the front seat of the septic-tank truck whittling with his knife on a treebranch. His open bag is sitting on the seat beside him. There is a box of nine-millimeter cartridges in the bag and he takes one of the cartridges out and compares the diameter of the bullet to the diameter of the stick he is whittling. Now he cuts a ring around the branch about three inches from the end.

The man climbs down from the cab of the truck and walks back and jams the end of the stick into the hole in the truck. He breaks off the branch and throws it to one side and folds away his knife and wipes his hands on his trousers and taps the plug in more firmly with the pistol and then goes back and climbs painfully up into the cab and shuts the door and rests for a minute with his eyes closed. Then he takes out his cell phone and dials a number and puts the phone to his ear.

WOUNDED MAN   Bueno. Tenemos la troca.

No. Más tiempo.

Por la mañana. Creo que sí.

Sí. A las siete, cómo no.

Problemas? No. Nada de importancia. Ándale pues.

He folds away the phone and rests for a few seconds. Then he starts the truck and drives up out of the ditch and the truck pulls away down the road, the gears shifting.

* * * * *

The woman with the red umbrella is walking up the street in the rain. A black Escalade pulls up alongside her splashing her with water from the gutter and two men get out. They come from behind with a cloth bag that has a leather belt around it and they pull this over her head and down almost to her knees and one of

*them pulls the strap and it draws shut instantly about her. They
then pick her up by the belt at either side and literally throw her
into the rear seat of the vehicle and shut the door and get in and
drive away leaving her purse and her poodle and her umbrella
on the sidewalk in the rain. Elapsed time about fifteen seconds.*

* * * * *

*The counselor is in the handicapped booth of the mens room at
an international airport talking on a cell phone.*

LAURA   I'm really worried, Baby.

COUNSELOR   It's going to be all right. I'll call you.

LAURA   Cant you meet me someplace?

COUNSELOR   I cant.

LAURA   That's not possible. That you cant.

COUNSELOR   God I miss you.

LAURA   Meet me.

COUNSELOR   We really have to be careful.

LAURA   You said that if they were looking for
               you they would have already found you.
               Isnt that what you said?

COUNSELOR   No. Not exactly.

LAURA   How bad is it? Baby?

Silence.

COUNSELOR   All right. Where.

LAURA   You say.

COUNSELOR   Alpha Centauri.

LAURA   That's too far. We'd be too old to do it. How about Boise?

COUNSELOR   Boise?

LAURA   Boise.

COUNSELOR   Why Boise?

LAURA   What's wrong with Boise?

COUNSELOR   Have you ever been to Boise?

LAURA   No. Have you?

COUNSELOR   No. What will you be wearing?

LAURA   A red dress.

COUNSELOR   What else?

LAURA   That's all.

COUNSELOR   No knickers.

LAURA   No.

COUNSELOR   Boise.

LAURA   Yes.

COUNSELOR   Do you have a hotel?

LAURA   I'm looking as we speak.

COUNSELOR   Wednesday.

LAURA   Tomorrow.

COUNSELOR   Wednesday. Leave me a message at the Delta Counter.

LAURA   I love you.

COUNSELOR   I love you.

The counselor folds the phone and drops it into the toilet and flushes it.

* * * * *

Plywood office of a junkyard in the desert. The junkyard man is talking on the phone. A pitbull lying on a mat at the side of his desk growls and stands up. The man looks up.

JUNKYARD MAN Tengo un cliente.

He hangs up the phone and looks at the client. The client comes forward in his bloodstained clothes and limps to a stop and reaches into his jacket. The junkyard man looks somewhat alarmed. The dog growls.

WOUNDED MAN Está bien. No le preocupe.

He takes a false-leather pouch with a bank logo from his coat and unzips it and takes out three banded sheafs of hundred-dollar bills and drops them onto the desk. The junkyard man stands up.

JUNKYARD MAN Cállete, Dulcinea. Cállete.

The dog lies down, grousing.

JUNKYARD MAN Siempre las más feroces, las perras.

The junkyard. The junkyard man is harrying two boys.

JUNKYARD MAN Ándale. Pronto! Pronto!

JUNKYARD BOY Pero es un pickup.

JUNKYARD MAN Sí, sí. Claro. Es lo mismo. Sólo la
frente es diferente. La cabina es
la misma. La cabina y las puertas.
Ándale.

*They run out through the lot, carrying a battered-looking
toolbox.*

*The septic-tank truck, parked in the junkyard lot. One of the
doors—bullet-riddled—is off and is standing against the front
wheel of the truck. A boy is unscrewing the other door with an
electric screwdriver while a second boy holds the door open. The
door is propped up on a crate with a two-by-four under its bottom edge and the second boy levers it up to take the weight off it.
It falls away and the two boys catch it and take it off and stand
it in the weeds against a wrecked car. The driver's door has exit
holes and the passenger door entry holes—and more of them.*

*The junkyard. The two boys with the toolbox catch the door
they've removed from a pickup truck and carry it down
past the rows of wrecked cars to the septic-tank truck.*

*The junkyard. The doorless septic-tank truck is being jacked
up on one side with two floor jacks. The junkyard man oper-
ates one of the jacks. The plug has been removed from the hole
in the tank and the sewage is leaking from the hole.*

JUNKYARD MAN Más atrás. Más.

The truck tilts up and the leak slows and then stops.

Junkyard. The owner is standing in a chair with welding goggles on and holding an oxyacetylene torch. He melts lead from a stick and spreads it over the bullethole in the tank with a wooden paddle.

Septic-tank truck. Two girls are scrubbing out the cab with brushes and pails of water. The seat is out of the truck. One of the doors has been put on and the junkyard man swings it shut and opens it again and adjusts the latch with a screwdriver. One of the boys is spray-painting the other door where it stands against some stacked parts with the window down.

A mobile home at the edge of the junkyard. A car pulls up in the drive and a woman gets out carrying a red plastic toolbox. She climbs the stairs where a girl holds the door for her.

Interior mobile home. The wounded man is lying on a cheap sofa with his leg stretched out on a coffeetable that is covered with a sheet. There is a plastic bucket in the floor with bloody gauze. The woman finishes wrapping his leg and turns and takes a syringe from her toolbox and unwraps it.

Reiner's house. Malkina's bedroom.

MALKINA   *(On the telephone)* Look. The last I heard they had just gone through Midland Texas. That was about twelve hours ago. Since then nothing. So I picked

up the phone and called the sheriff
and asked him if they had found any
dead bodies along the highway down
there and he said yes they had and
I thanked him and hung up. I know
you think I'm kidding. I'm not kidding.
And I'm not out. And I'm not kidding about that either. And yes. I know
where the truck is. All right. Really?
Well I think that falls under the cate-
gory of tough shit. We're all done here.

She hangs up the telephone.

* * * * *

*City street at night. A light rain is falling. Reiner in the white
Cadillac Escalade. The two cheetahs are in the rear. A black
Escalade pulls past and turns in front of him and cuts him
off and stops. Reiner hits the brakes and jams the gearshift
into reverse and turns to back up, his arm over the back of the
seat. The cheetahs are slammed about. Another Escalade pulls
in behind him and he slams the shifter back into drive again
and cuts the wheel to try to pull around the Escalade in front
of him but it has backed up and he is trapped between the two
vehicles. The driver has jumped out of the front Escalade and
he comes to Reiner's window and slams a prybar against it
but it only bounces off the glass. He slams it again. A second
man comes up and waves him away and jams a device against
the door that looks a bit like a shop router. He pulls down a
lever over the top of the machine and it fires a plunger into*

*the door with a sound like a pistol shot and he pushes another
lever up and pulls the door open with the device still attached.
He reaches in and grabs Reiner by the collar and pulls him
half way out of the vehicle. Reiner claws at his trouserleg and
comes up with a short barreled revolver from an ankle-holster.*

MAN WITH PRYBAR   Cuidado!

*The man pulling Reiner from his vehicle drops him and leaps
back and pulls an automatic pistol from the rear of his belt.
Reiner fires wildly and the man fires three rounds into Reiner
and Reiner slides out to lie face down in the street. His gun
clatters away. The man with the automatic pistol half turns
away and bangs the sides of his head with the heels of his fists
in frustration. The man with the prybar throws up his hands.*

MAN WITH PISTOL   Madre de Jesus! Hijo de puta!

*He kicks the dead man in the head and turns. He throws one
hand up in the air.*

MAN WITH PRYBAR   Vámanos.

*The man with the pistol shoves the gun into the back of his belt
and pulls up the lever on the doorjacker and pulls it away and
turns and kicks the corpse again.*

MAN WITH PISTOL   Pendejo.

*The two men turn and go back to the Escalade and get in and
pull away. The Escalade blocking Reiner's vehicle at the rear*

pulls past and follows and they disappear down the street in the rain. The two cheetahs at the rear window of the vehicle move to the side and sit looking out. A few people come forward from the surrounding buildings and stand looking. Two teenagers who are watching run out into the street and one takes Reiner's gun and the other his wristwatch and they take his billfold and turn him over face up and search the inside pockets of his coat and then they disappear in the rain. Reiner is lying face up in the street with the rain falling into his eyes.

* * * * *

City street in the rain. Night. Reiner is lying face up in the rain beneath the open door of the Escalade and the two cheetahs are crouched at either side of him and looking about furtively. One of them nudges Reiner's body with its nose.

* * * * *

Counselor on phone at his condominium.

COUNSELOR   I didnt think I'd reach you. Do you know where Reiner is?

WESTRAY   No.

COUNSELOR   He doesnt answer his cell and the phone at the club doesnt even ring.

WESTRAY   The club's closed. Some of Reiner's little friends showed up looking for

him and it wound up with them rough-
ing up some of the customers. All the
help ran out the back door. The cats
are gone. So that's pretty much that. I
mean if you wanted to get shot having
dinner you could just go to Juarez.

COUNSELOR   When was this?

WESTRAY   Two nights ago.

COUNSELOR   Have you talked to him?

WESTRAY   Yes.

COUNSELOR   What did he say?

WESTRAY   He said he was going to try and find
his cats. Before some dumb fucking
cop shot them—his words. They've got
these electronic tracking collars but
they can cover a hell of a lot of ground
in pretty short order. Where are you?

COUNSELOR   I'm home.

WESTRAY   I'm surprised you're still there.

COUNSELOR   I wont be in an hour.

WESTRAY   An hour.

COUNSELOR   Yeah.

WESTRAY   Well, you might want to think about whether you should loll around there all that long.

COUNSELOR   Where are you?

WESTRAY   I'm not at home.

Silence.

COUNSELOR   All right. I'm just going to throw some things in the car.

WESTRAY   In the car.

COUNSELOR   Yeah.

WESTRAY   What are you? A mental defective?

The counselor goes to the window and looks out.

COUNSELOR   What am I supposed to drive?

WESTRAY   I cant advise you, Counselor. Call a cab.

Silence.

WESTRAY   You're pretty quiet.

COUNSELOR   Yeah.

WESTRAY   Let me tell you something, Counselor.
                 If your description of a friend is some-
                 one who will die for you then you dont
                 have any friends. All right. I've got
                 to go.

COUNSELOR   All right.

WESTRAY   You take care now.

COUNSELOR   Yeah.

The phone clicks to dial tone.

*   *   *   *   *

Back yard of a suburban middle class home. The two chee-
tahs are walking along the edge of the swimming pool. One
stops to sniff at the water. In the pool are two boys, aged eight
and ten. They stand frozen. A man reclining in a poolside
canvas chair lowers the paper he is reading to see what the
silence is about. He freezes, holding the paper at the level
of his chest. The cheetahs amble slowly along the edge of the
pool and out across the lawn. The man lowers the paper into
his lap. The two boys turn to look at him. The oldest turns
to look where the cheetahs have gone and turns to the man
again.

BOY   Dad?

The man closes his eyes and raises one hand palm-out. Almost as if in blessing.

* * * * *

International Airport. Laura gets out of a rental car at the airport rental parking lot and pulls her bag over her shoulder and takes her suitcase off of the passenger seat and shuts the door.

Laura coming down the aisle of the parking lot trailing her suitcase on wheels behind her. A black Escalade is coming down the row behind her. At the end of the row of cars another Escalade pulls in front of her and stops. Two men get out. She turns but the other Escalade has pulled up behind her. She drops the handle of her suitcase and turns to run between the parked cars but a man seizes her by the arm and pushes her back toward the vehicle. She is struggling furiously but the other man grabs her hair and pulls her around and opens a switchblade knife in her face and she stops and lowers her head.

* * * * *

An upscale hotel room, king size bed, flowers in a vase on the dresser. Night. The counselor is at the window looking out at the rain.

Entrance to the hotel. The counselor is standing looking out at the street.

DOORMAN   Sir? Did you need a cab?

COUNSELOR   No. Thank you. I'm all right.

Hotel bar. The counselor is sitting at a small table in the corner. The waiter passes his table and stops.

WAITER   You all right here Sir?

COUNSELOR   Sorry?

WAITER   Can I bring you something?

COUNSELOR   No. Thank you.

The waiter turns to go and then turns back.

WAITER   Are you all right Sir?

The counselor looks up at the waiter.

COUNSELOR   Will you do something for me?

WAITER   Yessir. Of course.

The counselor takes out his billfold and takes out a card and hands it to the waiter.

COUNSELOR   That's my card. I'm a guest at the hotel. What I wish you would do for me is go to the desk and see if I have any messages. I know you're wondering why I dont go myself. But I've bothered them so much I think they're beginning to figure me for some sort of nutcase and I'm afraid they'll stop looking.

WAITER   *(Taking the card)* You got it.

* * * * *

Hotel room. Boise, Idaho.

COUNSELOR   Baby, please answer. Please answer. I dont know where you are. And if I dont know where you are I dont know where I am. I dont. I was lost all my life. I cant be lost again. I cant, Baby. I cant. The world without you is nothing. Just nothing.

* * * * *

Law office. Juarez Mexico. The counselor and a Mexican attorney or abogado. He is seated at his desk, his crocodile boots crossed on the desk top. He looks thoughtful. The counselor sits waiting.

ABOGADO   *(Mexican accent)* All right. I will have to make a call. You understand. Then if it is all right it is all right. Dont put me in the center. Okay?

COUNSELOR   In the middle.

ABOGADO   In the middle. Yes.

COUNSELOR   What do I owe you.

ABOGADO   You owe me nothing, Counselor. We are friends. A handshake. Wait for me. Have a coffee. I will have a yes or a no.

The counselor rises and reaches across the desk. The abogado rises. They shake hands.

COUNSELOR   Thank you.

The counselor turns to go.

ABOGADO   Counselor.

COUNSELOR   *(Turning)* Yes.

ABOGADO   I will do what I can do. But you must know that this is the long shot.

COUNSELOR   Yes. I do. Thank you.

ABOGADO   You're not—what do you call it? In hiding?

COUNSELOR   No. I was hiding. Now I'm seeking.

ABOGADO   Of course.

COUNSELOR   Thank you.

The abogado nods.

* * * * *

The counselor on the phone in a hotel room in El Paso.

JEFE   *(Spanish accent)* Yes. But I can only tell you what I told our friend. That there is no one to talk to.

COUNSELOR   Could I come to the Florída?

JEFE   The Florída is closed.

COUNSELOR   I would do whatever you suggest.

JEFE   But I have nothing to suggest, Counselor.

COUNSELOR   We could meet someplace.

JEFE   We are meeting now.

COUNSELOR   There must be someone I could see.

JEFE	I am afraid that there is no longer such a person. That is a thing of the past. I am afraid that there is no one to see.
COUNSELOR	Please dont hang up.
JEFE	I have some time. It is all right. I am just having my lunch.
COUNSELOR	There are people there?
JEFE	There is no one here. The waiter. I enjoy to have my lunch alone. It is more peaceful.
COUNSELOR	I'm not sure that you understand my position.
JEFE	But I do, Counselor. I lost a son. Two years ago. I thought that someone would call. To demand money. But there was no call. I never saw my son again. He was sixteen.
COUNSELOR	I'm sorry.
JEFE	Where the bodies are buried in the desert is a certain world, Counselor. Where they are simply left in the street is another. That is a country hereto-

fore unknown to me. But it must have always been here, must it not?

COUNSELOR   I dont know.

JEFE   Sí, sí. Con hielo, por favor. I'm sorry. You were saying.

The counselor is clutching the phone and leaning with the heel of his hand against his forehead, his eyes closed. He opens his eyes.

COUNSELOR   I dont know what I was saying.

JEFE   People are waiting. For what? At some point you must acknowledge that this new world is at last the world itself. There is not some other world. It is not merely a he ate us.

COUNSELOR   Hiatus.

JEFE   I'm sorry.

COUNSELOR   Hiatus. I believe the word is hiatus.

JEFE   Hiatus. Thank you, Counselor.

Silence.

COUNSELOR   Will you help me?

JEFE	I would urge you to see the truth of your situation, Counselor. That is my advice. It is not for me to say what you should have done. Or not done. I only know that the world in which you seek to undo your mistakes is not the world in which they were made. You are at a cross in the road and here you think to choose. But here there is no choosing. There is only accepting. The choosing was done long ago.

Silence.

JEFE	Are you there, Counselor?
COUNSELOR	Yes.
JEFE	I dont mean to upset you, but reflective men often find themselves at a certain remove from the realities of life. In any case, to prepare a place in our lives for the tragedies to come is an economy few wish to practice. Do you know the works of Antonio Machado?
COUNSELOR	No. I know his name.
JEFE	A lovely poet. I think his work does not translate so well. But the spanish is very beautiful. He was a schoolteacher

and he married a very beautiful young girl whom he loved very much. And she died. And so he became a great poet.

COUNSELOR I'm not going to become a great poet.

JEFE Perhaps not. But even were you to do so, it would be of little help to you. Machado would have given every line he wrote for one more hour with his beloved. There is no rule of exchange here, you see. Grief transcends every value. A man would give whole nations to lift it from his heart. And yet with it you can buy nothing.

Silence. The counselor holds his wrist to his forehead, his eyes closed.

JEFE When my son was lost to me I would not pray for that which I should most fervently have wished for. I could not.

COUNSELOR A speedy death.

JEFE I'm sorry.

COUNSELOR Why are you telling me this?

JEFE Because you stand at that crossing of which we spoke. You may dedicate your life to grief or not. The choice is yours. The assassin would claim you as well, but he will require your compliance. And of course he puts nothing of himself at hazard. He seeks to know what the warrior knows, but he has no stomach for the warrior's way. He is a usurper and a pimp. And as he is without courage he is greatly to be feared. He would explore that realm to which we are all consigned, but his way is to send an emissary. To bring his victim to the edge of the precipice with the greatest care and then lean to inquire if there be any news. Some word amid the sobbing. Amid the bleeding and the cries and the terror. Not even in the act of love will one be the object of such solicitude and such care.

COUNSELOR   Why are you telling me this?

JEFE   Because you cannot accept the reality of your life.

COUNSELOR   Why do you care?

JEFE   Do you love your wife so completely that you would take her place upon the wheel? Not die for her. That is easy.

But that your nerve would not fail you
as they bend to buckle the straps?

COUNSELOR   Yes. Yes, damn you.

Silence.

JEFE   That is good to hear, Counselor.

COUNSELOR   What are you saying? Are you saying
                that this is possible?

JEFE   No. It is not possible. Sí. Un cafecito.
                Por favor. Negro. Negro, sí. Gracias.
                I'm sorry, Counselor.

COUNSELOR   You said I was that man. At that cross-
                ing.

JEFE   Yes. At the understanding that life will
                not take you back. I have no wish to
                paint the world in colors more som-
                ber than those it wears, but as the
                world gives way to darkness it becomes
                more and more difficult to dismiss the
                understanding that the world is in fact
                oneself. It is a thing which you have
                created, no more, no less. And when
                you cease to be so will the world. There
                will be other worlds. Of course. But
                they are the worlds of other men and

your understanding of them was never more than an illusion anyway. Your world—the only one that matters—will be gone. And it will never come again. The extinction of all reality is a concept no resignation can encompass. Until annihilation comes. And all grand ideas are seen for what they are. And now I must go. I have calls to make, and then, if there is time, I will take a little nap.

The phone rings off.

* * * * *

Night. Malkina and the black weightlifter are driving through the outskirts of the city. She is sitting with a GPS and a tracking monitor for the transponder. A narrow two-lane blacktop road in the headlights. Some lights in the distance. They come to a crossroads and the weight-lifter slows and looks at her.

MALKINA   Left. Go left.

They drive slowly along the road. Suddenly one of the cheetahs crosses the road ahead of them in the lights.

MALKINA   (*Almost crying*) It's Silvia. Hi, Baby. Hi, Baby.

* * * * *

A garage, the septic-tank truck. There is a gantry crane over-head—a chain hoist that slides on iron rails—and a man in coveralls and welding glasses is slicing open the tank of the truck laterally from front to rear with a cutting torch.

Garage. A welder is on top of the tank welding a metal bar to the tank. There is a heavy metal hook bolted through the bar and a similar hook is already in place toward the front of the truck. He finishes and tips up his mask and stands and pulls the hoist toward him along the rails with its chains swinging.

Garage. The top half of the tank is being lifted by the two hooks and the chains from the single hook hanging from the pulley. Inside the severed tank lie four fifty-five gallon steel drums. The gantry crane moves down the rail and lowers the top of the tank to the concrete floor behind the truck and a worker—in coveralls and wearing a mask—unhooks the chains and then the gantry moves back over the truck and he hooks a crosschain to the first of the barrels and tightens it with its turnbuckle and the first of the drums is lifted out of the tank.

The washbay in the corner of the garage. The four drums are standing upright on pallets and the worker in coveralls and rubber boots is hosing them down with a steamwasher.

* * * * *

Streets of Juarez. There is a yellow police ribbon strung across sawhorses blocking off the street and in the middle distance is a car that has been machinegunned. One door is open and there is a dead body in the street. Police cars with their roof-lights strobing. In the foreground people are marching with signs and with banners. They contain large full color portraits of the missing. The signs say: Desaparecido, or Desaparecido with a date following. They say: Se Busca A with a name following. Some of the women carry umbrellas against the sun and some carry crosses of raw wood and crosses with wreaths mounted on them. A khaki-colored Army jeep with a soldier in battle-dress at the rear of a mounted machinegun fords its way through the crowd. The counselor is among the mourners, carrying a poster with a color photograph of Laura.

* * * * *

Three men in breathing masks at the washbay. One is in workclothes and one is in white coveralls. The third, well dressed in slacks and sportcoat, is the Buyer. The worker has an electric driver and is unfastening the tops of the drums. One of them is already open and the man in coveralls takes out four clear plastic bags each holding a kilo of cocaine. The worker unscrews the bolt on the second drum and lifts away the rim that circles the top of the drum and then lifts away the top of the drum and moves on to the next drum. The buyer follows the man in coveralls across the garage. They have removed their masks.

BUYER   Why are there four drums?

COVERALL MAN   *(Mexican accent)* I dont know. I think maybe we have a traveler.

BUYER   A traveler?

COVERALL MAN   Yes. A free rider. How do you say?
               Like you have on a ship. A some-
               thing away.

BUYER   A stowaway?

COVERALL MAN   Yes. A stowaway.

WORKMAN   Madre de Jesus!

*The coverall man turns, smiling. The workman has left the
washbay and he has pulled away his mask and is almost gag-
ging.*

WORKMAN   Son of a beetch!

COVERALL MAN   Cierrelo! Pronto! Pronto!

*He turns and goes through a metal door, laughing. The Buyer
follows him up a set of concrete steps, iron pipe railing.*

*A small office with a glass window looking down to where the
septic-tank truck is parked. Coverall man and the Buyer are
sitting at a cheap metal table. There are computers on the
table. A scale and some plates and the plastic bags of cocaine.*

BUYER   In the last two accounts we're only
               an hour different. But it's another
               day. It's tomorrow.

COVERALL MAN	Yes. I love that.
BUYER	We're okay. We have what? Four hours?
COVERALL MAN	Yes. Perhaps we should know if electronic money earns an extra day of interest when it crosses the International Date Line.
BUYER	Good question. Why do they send you a dead body?
COVERALL MAN	No reason. It is convenient.
BUYER	Convenient.
COVERALL MAN	Yes. There is always somebody you wish for him to go away. So you send him to America.
BUYER	Do you know who he is?
COVERALL MAN	No. Of course not. He is a pasajero.
BUYER	A passenger?
COVERALL MAN	Yes. An immigrant.
BUYER	It's just a way to get rid of a body.

COVERALL MAN   Yes. Just a way. Somebody you dont want around.

BUYER   From Mexico.

COVERALL MAN   From Colombia.

BUYER   He came from Colombia.

COVERALL MAN   Yes. Of course.

BUYER   What will you do with him?

COVERALL MAN   Nothing. He goes back in the truck.

BUYER   He goes back in the truck.

COVERALL MAN   Of course.

BUYER   And then what?

COVERALL MAN   Nothing. It is normal. Well. Not so normal I suppose. They think it is funny. A sort of joke. You have to have a sense of humor in this business.

BUYER   So what happens to him?

COVERALL MAN   Nothing. The truck goes back together. They paint it. He is inside.

He rides around. Maybe they sell the truck. At auction maybe. It's all the same. He rides around some more. Sucking up the shit. Welcome to America.

He smiles broadly. He checks the time by his Rolex.

* * * * *

A cafe in a border town. The counselor is lying at one of the cheap formica tables with his head in his folded arms, the photograph poster of Laura on the table.

CAFE MAN   Señor.

COUNSELOR   Yes.

CAFE MAN   Señor.

The counselor sits up and looks at the man.

CAFE MAN   I must close.

COUNSELOR   I know.

The counselor is haggard and unshaven.

CAFE MAN   What you do? You have place to go maybe.

COUNSELOR   You dont have to go home but you cant stay here.

CAFE MAN   Cómo?

COUNSELOR   It's all right.

The counselor rises, picking up the photograph.

COUNSELOR   I fell asleep. I'm sorry.

CAFE MAN   There is no harm.

COUNSELOR   No harm. Lovely thought. Magical thought.

CAFE MAN   Cómo?

COUNSELOR   Good night.

FE MAN   Es muy peligroso. En las calles.

SELOR   I know.

CAF

N   They hear somebody in the street they shoot them. Then they turn on the light to see who is dead.

COUNSELOR   Why do they do that?

CAFE MAN	*(Shrugging)* To make a joke. To show that death does not care. That death has no meaning.
COUNSELOR	Qué piensa? Usted. Do you believe that?
CAFE MAN	No. Of course not. All my family is dead. I am the one who has no meaning.
COUNSELOR	Entiendo.
CAFE MAN	Cuidado. Sí?
COUNSELOR	Sí. Cuidado.
CAFE MAN	Quién es? La Señora.
COUNSELOR	*(Turning at the door)* Mi esposa.
CAFE MAN	Ah. Guapa. Lo siento.

The counselor stands at the door.

COUNSELOR	Sí. Guapa. What is that?
CAFE MAN	It means she is beautiful.
COUNSELOR	No. I mean what does that mean? What is it? Beautiful.

CAFE MAN   I dont know. It is late.

COUNSELOR   Yes. Good night.

CAFE MAN   Good night, Amigo. Good night.

* * * * *

*The counselor goes down an alley to a door and takes out a
key and lets himself in. A bleak hallway, linoleum floor. A
lightbulb hanging from the ceiling. He lets himself in at the
first door on the right and turns on the light. A room with an
iron bed and a cheap dresser and a sink. He fastens the chain
and crosses to the bed and sits. He puts his poster on the bed
beside him and lowers his face into his hands. Machinegun
fire briefly in the distance.*

* * * * *

*International Airport. Westray exits carrying a medium-
sized bag and a shoulder bag. He is dressed in a dark suit. He
stands at the curb studying the cabs and limousines and then
he crosses the street to a black town car and opens the door
and gets in. The driver is an attractive woman who wears a
chauffeur's cap. She turns and smiles at him.*

WESTRAY   Me gusta su sombrero.

CHAUFFEUR   Thank you.

WESTRAY   The International.

CHAUFFEUR   *(Smiling)* I know.

She turns and starts the engine and they pull out into the traffic.

* * * * *

Desk at a major hotel in a world city. Westray is standing at the counter with his passport and credit card. He is waiting while the clerk checks his reservation. A very attractive blonde is standing a few feet away, checking in. She is dressed in a dark business suit and carries a large shoulder bag. Westray looks her over. She glances at him.

WESTRAY   How are you doing?

BLONDE   Okay. You're Canadian.

WESTRAY   You saw my passport. Where are you from?

BLONDE   New Mexico.

WESTRAY   Have a drink with me.

BLONDE   What?

WESTRAY   Have a drink with me. You're not married.

BLONDE   No.

WESTRAY   Get checked in. We can sit right over
               there. They'll bring us whatever we
               want.

BLONDE   You're a masher.

WESTRAY   A masher? Lord. Where did you hear
               that?

BLONDE   I'm teasing. I think.

WESTRAY   I'm a very decent chap. You'll see.

BLONDE   Do you have any references?

WESTRAY   Mmm. This is getting better all the
               time.

* * * * *

World city. Malkina, dressed in a business suit, is crossing the
street. She walks down the sidewalk to a jeweler's window and
stands looking at the display behind the glass.

Sidewalk cafe in the city. Malkina is looking at a scrap of
paper and talking to the blonde from the hotel desk.

MALKINA   Five digits. Who's Rowena?

BLONDE	I dont know.
MALKINA	Social. His driver's license is Nevada?
BLONDE	Yes.
MALKINA	All right. Your little bonus is in an envelope in my purse.

The Blonde opens one of two purses on the table and takes out the envelope and puts it in the other purse.

BLONDE	You still wont have his computer.
MALKINA	I'll have the computer. Were you planning on seeing him again?
BLONDE	What would be the point? He'll be broke.
MALKINA	Smart girl.
BLONDE	Or is it worse than that?
MALKINA	What do you care?
BLONDE	I dont want to get mixed up in something heavy.
MALKINA	You already are.

BLONDE   How do you mean?

MALKINA   What if he were to come looking for you?

BLONDE   But he wont. Will he?

MALKINA   No. He wont.

The Blonde sits staring at the sidewalk.

BLONDE   Oh, Jesus.

She gets up and takes her purse and takes out the envelope and puts it on the table.

MALKINA   What's that?

BLONDE   I dont want it.

MALKINA   Dont be a sap.

BLONDE   I cant. I have to go.

MALKINA   Well. Please yourself. You know what I like about Americans?

BLONDE   *(Blinking back the tears, angry)* No. What?

MALKINA   *(Smiling)* You can depend on them.

* * * * *

Morning. The counselor is asleep on the cot with his clothes on. There is a knocking at the door. He sits up. The knocking again.

COUNSELOR   Momento. Momento.

He crosses the room and undoes the chain and opens the door. A young man is standing there holding a package.

DELIVERY BOY   Está el abogado?

COUNSELOR   Sí.

The boy hands him the package and smiles and touches his cap and turns to go.

COUNSELOR   Momento. Qué es este?

The boy is at the outer door. He turns and holds out both hands.

DELIVERY BOY   Yo no sé. Un regalo. Quién sabe? Ábralo.

The boy goes out. The counselor goes back into his room and sits on the cot looking at the package. It is about five inches square and wrapped in paper and tied with a blue ribbon. He pulls the ribbon loose and it falls to the floor. He unwraps the paper and sits looking at a DVD. Suddenly he realizes what it is and he turns and drops it onto the bed like something hot and clutches at his face, his hands clawed.

COUNSELOR   Oh God. Oh God. Oh God.

* * * * *

A major street, world city. Westray comes out of a large building, possibly a bank. He is dressed in a tan summer business
suit and he is carrying a small black canvas bag. As he exits
into the street a man comes up behind him and drops the wire
of a bolito over his head and pulls the wire taut by its loop.
Westray instantly drops the bag and seizes the wire about his
neck and turns, wild-eyed. The assassin picks up the bag in
one movement and steps from the curb into the street where he
gets into a taxicab that is waiting for him with the door open.
The cab pulls away into the traffic.

Westray turning, the fingers of one hand caught in the wire
now being severed and the wire drawing into his neck. His
collar is red with blood. He sits down on the pavement and
kicks his feet, as if in annoyance. Almost like a petulant child.
Pedestrians have begun to stop, although at a distance. The
gearmotor of the bolito is grinding. Westray falls over, kick-
ing. His left carotid artery bursts and bright red blood sprays
in a fountain into the air and splashes back on the sidewalk.
The spectators draw back.

Inside the cab Malkina is sitting in the back seat with the
assassin. She takes the case and puts it in her lap and unzips
it and sorts through it. She takes out a computer and she looks
through the papers in a folder. She unzips a pocket in the case
and takes out a pair of passports. She takes out an envelope. A
jump drive. She puts all these things in her shoulder bag and
takes out an envelope and hands it to the assassin and he puts

it in his shirt and she zips shut her shoulder bag and leans and taps the cabdriver on the shoulder.

MALKINA   Aquí, por favor.

CABDRIVER   Aquí?

MALKINA   Sí.

The cab pulls to the curb and Malkina hands the driver some bills and gets out and shuts the door. The cabdriver looks at the money and purses his mouth in surprise and approval. He turns to the man in the back.

CABDRIVER   A dónde?

The assassin is watching Malkina as she disappears among the pedestrians. Her elegant fitted clothes.

* * * * *

Sidewalk cafe. World city. Malkina at a table with Lee—a twenty-five-year-old Chinese American.

LEE   What do you have? Do you have the CAs?

MALKINA   I have two of them.

LEE   Can you get the other two?

MALKINA	Yes. I've got a search engine download-ing them out of another computer.
LEE	There's another player.
MALKINA	No. He's out of the picture.
LEE	How far out?
MALKINA	All the way out.
LEE	You're sure.
MALKINA	Very sure.

Lee studies her.

LEE	Do you ever get a sudden dark feeling about something?
MALKINA	Concerning a deal?
LEE	Concerning anything.
MALKINA	I dont know. But I could imagine that my dark and your dark are different darks.
LEE	All right.

MALKINA   I'll have everything by tomorrow that
              there is to get. What we dont have we'll
              just have to figure out. I've got the routing
              numbers and the account numbers. I've
              got the source code but we'll have to have
              a compiler to translate everything into
              machine-readable code. It's all doable.

LEE   VPNs and routers.

MALKINA   Yes.

LEE   Passwords.

MALKINA   What is it you really want to know?

LEE   There's somebody else. Your bank guy?

MALKINA   He gets ten percent and all his costs
              come out of his end.

LEE   Are you Ukrainian?

MALKINA   No. Soy pura Porteña.

LEE   All right.

MALKINA   You dont have to worry about my con-
              nections. I'm an independent operator.

LEE	I worry about everything. That's why I'm still in business. This is basically a spoof.
MALKINA	If you like.
LEE	All right. What is it that *you* want to know?
MALKINA	I'd like to know how clean you are.
LEE	I dont keep anything around that I dont have to.
MALKINA	Yes. Well you can have a basic tool kit with Sequel servers and whatever but a remote access Trojan Horse like Zrizbi or Torig is not for keeping track of your household expenses.
LEE	It's not illegal to own one.
MALKINA	That's not the point. When they find it they keep looking.
LEE	Okay.
MALKINA	You can clone your cell phone with a SIM writer but the bills keep going to the number you're cloned off of so you cant use it forever.

LEE   We dont want to use it forever.

MALKINA   I know. But you dont know how much
               time you have. Forever can be pretty
               fucking short. Plus hackers think you
               cant trace a cloned cell phone but that's
               not really true any more. And if they get
               a trace they can use a Stingray and locate
               you physically to within about five feet.
               You dont want that in your life.

LEE   All right. How many calls total, four?

MALKINA   Yes.

LEE   Voice crypt.

MALKINA   Yes. Separate shoes.

LEE   Yeah, well, on the subject of security I
               know that you understand nothing gets
               off the hard drive, but this would still
               come under the heading of time con-
               straints.

MALKINA   I'm not worried about that. What's out
               there is out there. They think their
               traffic analysis is sophisticated but by
               definition it has to lag the protocols
               that generate it. As for the physical
               computers you just put them in the

oven and set it to four-fifty and walk away. Everything I need to take with me I can download onto a USB stick.

LEE   Double encrypted.

MALKINA   Yes.

LEE   Random seed.

MALKINA   Yes.

LEE   All right. Let me look at it. We havent talked money.

MALKINA   Quarter mil.

LEE   I dont suppose you'd tell me what the caper is worth.

MALKINA   Why not? You're going to see it up on the screen anyway. It's twenty-two mill, give or take whatever. And if we nail all four accounts.

LEE   You could boot that quarter up a bit.

MALKINA   All right.

LEE   Five hundred K.

MALKINA	That's not a bit. That's double.
LEE	Four hundred.
MALKINA	Done.
LEE	Cash.
MALKINA	Cash. Do you need something up front?
LEE	No. I'm good. What are you going to do, float a bank loan?
MALKINA	Something like that.

* * * * *

City street. Ambulance siren. The ambulance pulls up onto the sidewalk where Westray is lying, parting the crowd. Three medics get out and go to the body and place a sheet over it and one of them takes a pulse at the wrist and then they get a gurney out of the ambulance and place it on the sidewalk and one of the medics picks up the body by the feet and the other two take hold at either side and they lift the body onto the gurney still covered by the sheet. A gasp goes up from the crowd and when the medics turn to look Westray's severed head is still lying on the sidewalk together with the bolito.

* * * * *

Landfill on the outskirts of Juarez. Bleak desert landscape with raw mountains hazy in the distance. Sound of a bulldozer. The landfill is a rubble of nameless trash. There are fires burning and smoke drifts across the fill. Families in the distance are picking through the garbage. Women and children. They carry woven shopping bags over their shoulders. A few buzzards strut about. An old ten-ton dumptruck labors across the landfill and turns and halts and backs and comes to a stop and the driver pulls the lever and the bed tips up and dumps its load of trash. The driver jiggles the lever and the bed clangs and then he lowers the bed into place and the truck lumbers away. A dusty yellow bulldozer pulls up and begins to grade the trash away into the fill. A girl's body comes up in the trash and then rolls under again. The bulldozer backs and then goes forward again. The headless body of Laura in her red dress appears briefly and then disappears in the trash and garbage.

*   *   *   *   *

World city, apartment in a high rise building. Night. The reflection of Lee's face in the glass. Reflection of a bank of computers behind him. The lights of the city below. Malkina crosses the room and then crosses back.

Lee and Malkina sitting at the computers. She is wearing a set of headphones. Lines of text running on the screens.

LEE   What's the time delay again?

MALKINA   *(Taking off headset)* What?

LEE   I'm just rattling your cage.

MALKINA   Dont.

LEE   All right.

Malkina brings tea from the kitchen. They sit at the screens.

MALKINA   We've got two hours.

LEE   You want to try and get some sleep? I'll
               wake you.

MALKINA   I'm too wired.

LEE   You want to go for a walk?

MALKINA   I'm not leaving this suite if the build-
               ing catches fire. You can see what's on
               television if you like.

LEE   What if it's us?

MALKINA   I dont know. Maybe they have virtual
               prisons for virtual felons.

* * * * *

Arizona high plains. The male cheetah is lying under a tree. He gets up and walks out to the edge of the grass and stands looking into the distance.

* * * * *

A penthouse restaurant in a major city at night, the lights of the city spread out below. Malkina is at the door being greeted by the maitre d'.

MAITRE D' Buena noches, Señora. Buena noches.

With her is a tall and elegant man in his forties dressed in a black business suit with an expensive gold silk tie. The maitre'd holds out his hand for them to enter.

MAITRE D' Bienvenidos. Bienvenidos.

She is dressed in an ankle-length black pleated skirt, a dark green bolero jacket with black braiding. She wears a heavy graduated swag choke necklace of emeralds with matching earrings. She is about five months pregnant, just noticeable. They cross through the room and the maitre'd gestures them to a window table where a waiter holds a chair for her. A second waiter is unfolding their napkins and a third is crossing the room with a champagne bucket on a pedestal which he positions at the man's elbow. He lifts a bottle of Dom Pérignon from the bucket and wraps it with a towel and twists out the cork and pours two flutes of the champagne and then twists the bottle back into the ice. The maitre d' bows.

MAITRE D'   Buen appetivo.

He moves away. They touch glasses. The escort speaks with an accent possibly European.

ESCORT   To the heir then.

MALKINA   Thank you.

ESCORT   Will you return to the States then? At that time?

MALKINA   I dont think so.

ESCORT   Where will you go?

MALKINA   I can go wherever I choose.

ESCORT   To Europe?

MALKINA   There's not going to be a Europe. I think I might like China.

ESCORT   China. Really?

MALKINA   Yes.

ESCORT   You dont speak the language.

MALKINA   *(Smiling)* I'm a quick study.

ESCORT   How do you get money into China?

MALKINA   It's not a problem. You can buy into
          the market. Heavy industries are good.
          Pohang Iron and Steel I like.

ESCORT   What about cash?

MALKINA   The easiest way to compress wealth is
          with diamonds. They're highly negotia-
          ble and they weigh nothing. Although a
          Picasso painting—out of the frame and
          rolled up—is worth about the same.
          Ounce for ounce.

ESCORT   And how much would that be?

MALKINA   (*Smiling*) Is this an idle curiosity?

ESCORT   It's a curiosity.

MALKINA   There are roughly a hundred and fifty
          carats in an ounce. And diamonds aver-
          age out to about ten thousand dollars
          a carat. Stones in the two to five carat
          range. Can you do the math?

ESCORT   You do it.

MALKINA   Diamonds are worth about one point
          five million an ounce. You can hold

twenty million dollars in the palm of your hand. Money itself weighs out at about three thousand dollars to the ounce. Roughly fifty thousand dollars a pound. So that twenty mil in your hand would be over four hundred pounds of paper in hundred-dollar bills. Four forty, to be exact.

ESCORT   Can you sell diamonds in China?

MALKINA   You can sell diamonds on Mars.

ESCORT   What if it's a girl? Wouldnt that be a problem?

MALKINA   It would. But he's not.

ESCORT   I see. May I ask you something?

MALKINA   You may ask.

ESCORT   Is the child Reiner's?

MALKINA   Is that what you want to know?

ESCORT   Yes.

MALKINA   No. It's not. Reiner had had a vasectomy. The counselor used to tell people that it was court-ordered. I told him the day that I found out. He was all right with it. He wanted me to get an abortion and we would go on as if nothing had happened. He was actually somewhat emotional about it. It surprised me. I told him that if it was a girl I would abort it. But it wasnt. And I didnt.

ESCORT   Did he want to know whose it was?

MALKINA   Of course.

ESCORT   Did you tell him?

MALKINA   No.

ESCORT   The child will have no father.

MALKINA   Every child has a father. In this case the best kind of father.

ESCORT   And what kind of father is that?

MALKINA   The best kind of father is a dead father.

ESCORT   You are serious.

MALKINA   I think that Freud is right in that a son who is worshipped by his mother will never doubt himself. But a contentious father can undo that. And the virtues of a dead father—his very identity for that matter—are limited only by the mother's imagination. You look a bit uncomfortable.

ESCORT   I'm fine.

MALKINA   If I were a woman that you could have, then you would not be interested. The curse of the player.

ESCORT   I hope that is not true.

MALKINA   (*Smiling*) No one wants to admit that the object of his desire has weighed him in the balance and found him wanting. That is a very hard thing to accept. Better to imagine the desired one as whimsical and irresolute. Would you agree?

ESCORT   (*Smiling*) You are quite cruel.

MALKINA   You will thank me.

ESCORT   What is it that *you* want?

MALKINA   My own life. I own very little. Some jewelry. A few clothes. There are times when I imagine that I would like my innocence back. If I ever had it. But I would never pay the price which it now commands on the market.

ESCORT   (*Nodding. Looking up at her. Quietly*) Your own life.

MALKINA   (*Studying him. Then*) When the world itself is the source of your torment then you are free to exact vengeance upon any least part of it. I think perhaps you would have to be a woman to understand that. And you will never know the depth of your hurt until you are presented with the opportunity for revenge. Only then will you know what you are capable of.

ESCORT   I think you have told me more than I wished to know.

MALKINA   It's all right.

ESCORT   And the cats?

MALKINA   Silvia died. She had a congenital heart condition. Which we knew. Raoul is alive and well in Arizona. He rules over a domain of a thousand hectares and he has a special rock where he can take the sun and watch for game. That's all. Dogs bring people together. Cats dont. Still, I miss him.

ESCORT   Raoul.

MALKINA   (Smiling) Yes. Raoul. I miss watching him bring down jackrabbits out on the desert at seventy miles an hour. I never tired of that. To see quarry killed with elegance is very moving to me. It always was.

ESCORT   Is it sexual?

MALKINA   Of course. A thing like that is always sexual. But grace. Freedom. The hunter has a purity of heart that exists nowhere else. I think he is not defined so much by what he has come to be as by all that he has escaped being. You can make no distinction between what he is and what he does. And what he does is kill. We of course are another matter. I suspect that we are ill-formed for the path we have chosen. Ill-formed and ill-prepared. We would like to draw a veil over all that blood and terror. That have brought us to this place. It is our faintness of heart that would close our eyes to all of that, but in so doing it makes of it our destiny. Perhaps you would not agree. I dont know. But nothing is crueller than a coward, and the slaughter to come is probably beyond our imagining. Should we think about ordering? I'm famished.

CREDITS